The Basics
of Boat Travel
with Your Cat or Dog

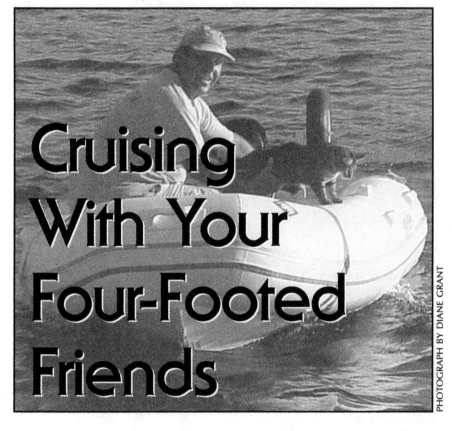

Cruising
With Your
Four-Footed
Friends

DIANA JESSIE

SEAWORTHY PUBLICATIONS, INC.
Port Washington, Wisconsin

Cruising With Your Four-Footed Friends

For rights inquiries, or to contact the publisher:
Seaworthy Publications, Inc.
215 S. Park St., Suite #1
Port Washington, WI 53074
Phone: 262-268-9250
Fax: 262-268-9208
e-mail: publisher@seaworthy.com
Visit us on the Web at: http://www.seaworthy.com

Library of Congress Cataloging-in-Publication Data

Jessie, Diana.
    Cruising with your four-footed friends : the basics of boat travel with your cat or dog /by Diana B. Jessie
        p. cm.
    Includes bibliographical references (p.).
    ISBN 1-892399-16-4 (alk. paper)
        1. Boating with dogs. 2. Boating with cats. 3. Pets and travel. I. Title.

SF427.456.J47 2003
636.088'7--dc21

2003045561

Cover design by Brian Murphy, Digital Dreamland
Cover photographs by Diane Grant and Janet Parks
Design and composition by John Reinhardt Book Design

Dedicated to Rudder and Tiller,
A precious pair whose memory makes us smile

Acknowledgments

Completing this book required the cooperation of numerous individuals, several organizations, and some formidable four-footed friends. First, I want to thank Jonathan Eaton of International Marine/McGraw Hill for permission to use material from Alvah Simon's *North to the Night*. Originally published by International Marine in 1998, the book is still available from Broadway Books in paperback. Clare Murphy made it possible to use the seeds of wisdom from Paul Kunkel's *How to Toilet Train Your Cat* published by Workman Press in 1991. Eric Brotman's photo of Mango, a completely trained cat, is an inspiration for those who look for freedom from the litter box. He gave us permission to use this photo from his book *How to Toilet Train Your Cat, the Education of Mango*, Bird Brain Press, Inc, in 2000. My husband and I took many photographs. Fortunately, we were permitted to use the photos of others. Friedrich Gross took the pictures of Tania Aebi and Tarzoon; Adam Loory took the picture of Polar the Wonder Cat; Rebecca Rhoades, DVM, in addition to being the executive director of the Humane Society in Kauai, took the pictures of Hokget; Jim Bingman shared his photos of Honey and her puppies; Les Sutton generously allowed us to use his slides of Cami; Janet and Blaine Parks interrupted their cruising to get their photos of Bailey and Max to us; Don Freeman did photos to order of Tristan and Marilee Schaffer persuaded Lola to model a PFD for the camera. Jim Forrest came through with pictures of his lab, Cassie. They filled in the critical gaps where we didn't have

My four-footed friends can't speak for themselves, but here is a gallery of some of the pets you will meet in the course of reading this book. From top to bottom (columns), left to right:

Bubba, a Burmese youngster learning about boats.
Hokget, a mixed terrier survivor who lived alone at sea for 24 days.
Chaucer, a Golden Retriever with a stylish attitude.
Boca, our 30,000-mile, multilingual crew.
Daisy, like her name, a delightful and very smart Airedale.
Zorba, whose short life doesn't diminish his place as our first feline crew.

Boris, an elegant giant Schnauzer with a heart to match.
Cami, a feline wise to cruising in Mexico.
Bailey, one of a matched pair of golden retrievers, cruising the Caribbean.
Cassie, who has passed water appreciation 101 for Labradors.
Ilia, saved by Falcon, this is a seagoing Jack Russell.
Cutter, a Schipperke with many miles and even more smarts.
Fawna, the tiniest of the tiny, toy terriers.

Honey, a yellow Labrador who survived and bore nine puppies.
Polar the Wonder Cat, a fuzzy Himalayan with a City Island accent.
Tarzoon, a happy tabby who has given up the sea.
Lola, every inch a lady when she isn't a brazen hussy.
Schooner, a well-traveled Persian out to see the world.
Max, Bailey's mate who loves life on *Charbonneau*.
Tristan, a standard black poodle that commutes between boats.

Foxy, our former water-cat, now a retired country boy.
Obi, the sweetest Lhasa Apso, whose gone cruising.
Murray, a terrier foundling with lots of attitude and great taste.
Sidney, a Golden Retriever with an insatiable appetite.
Mango, smarter than the average cat or two-year old.
Maggie, Bubba's mate, a Burmese with a very pushy attitude.
Tyler, an extraordinary German Shepherd (aren't they all?).

(not pictured) Tiller, Rudder, Suzette, Joliette, Avunga, Kili, Fili, Pooh, Piglet, Halifax, Neysa, Pearl, and Mancha were too busy sniffing the roses, chasing birds, or riding clouds to pose.

Collecting information on a wide range of subjects was a slow task. I received invaluable help finding my way through the maze from Terri Parrow of Boat U.S, David Madden of Ruff Wear, Shannon Zappala of King Arthur Flour, and Henry Marx of Landfall Navigation. Brian Sodergren, Issues Specialist with the Humane Society of the United States (HSUS) reviewed and contributed editing that helped me understand the position of HSUS on the protection of our pets' welfare. The quarantine offices were all helpful but Australia, Hawaii and the United Kingdom went the extra mile helping me to find the most current and definitive information. Special thanks to the Honolulu Quarantine station for letting me take pictures on a "closed" day. Jack Dausend gave me new and needed facts through Boaters' Enterprise, a special source with current quarantine information on Trinidad and Tobago.

Talking about pets is an immediate basis for new friendships, and I am the beneficiary. My new and special friends Christine and Dan Dowler, Karen and Tim Crowe, Andrew and Linda Fraser, Mike Ganahl and Leslie Hardy, Jaye Eldridge and Art Stiers, Rod and Cherie Williams, Ann Hoffner, Kay Malseed, Ann and Mike McDougall, Art and Nancy White, John and Barbara Martino, Janet and Blaine Parks, Don Freeman, and Jim Bingman were all willing to share stories and experiences. Old friends came to my rescue more than once including Adam Loory and Jenni Rodda, Mike, Karen, and Falcon Riley, Jim Forrest, and Marilee Shaffer.

Three well-known and experienced sailors told me some amazing pet stories that I have shared in the book. Robin Graham, the youngest solo circumnavigator, Tania Aebi, the youngest woman solo circumnavigator, and Alvah Simon of Arctic fame were generous with their time and enthusiastic about sharing their experiences.

Mary Iverson shared many giggles when we cruised with our cats, and I knew she would help. Her contributions were many and one was the saddest yet most worthwhile that I received. Losing her cats at sea gave a very different perspective to those cruising dreams we have.

Dr. Robert Evans, veterinarian and sailor extraordinaire, came to my rescue with help and suggestions about medical care and first aid for pets. His background and training combined with his sailing experience gave him the special perspective I needed. Trying to explain to a "land bound" veterinarian what life on a boat is like is almost too extreme to be grasped. Bob's years on the water combined with his professional success made him the ideal mentor.

Donna Green-Tye worked patiently editing, re-editing, and keeping me focused on you the reader. Her skill combined with her love of animals expanded my goals for the book. Her effort and long hours were significant in completing this book.

Thanks to Oscar Lind for introducing me to Seaworthy Publications who let me write about cats, dogs, and boats.

To my husband, Jim, who is my best friend and willingly puts up with my crazy hours, frequently cold coffee, taking hundreds of pictures of moving targets, and then making those images appear on the computer, I promise that there will be a puppy in your future.

CONTENTS

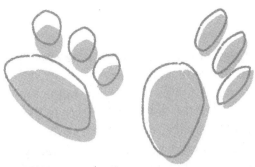

FOREWORD

Human history is inextricably tied with the many animal species with which we share our Earth. Their contribution to our success, even ascendancy in nature has not been merely that of fur, leather, meat and milk. Put in its simplest terms, the much-lauded "March Of Man" has been made upon the backs of beasts. When the scorching desert stretched ahead with no end in sight, only the hideous but hardy camel could carry the parched nomad through to oasis. The fleet footed horse set us free from our stumbling slowness to sweep like the wind over the amber plains. From the mightiest land mammal ripping teak logs from the equatorial forests for his Mahout, to the tiniest song-bird dropping from its perch in warning to the miners of the deep, we have made our long journey with the help of the leathered, feathered, and furred.

With the families *Canidae* and *Felidae*, dogs and cats, we formed a relationship that bordered more on partnership than ownership. The terms of this ancient pact were simple. For the dog, we agreed to provide a regular source of food, protection from competing packs, and a warm spot near the fire. In exchange for this and an occasional scratch behind the ear, they lent us their far keener senses of sight, smell, and hearing. Their eyes, ears and noses shaped our first Defense Early Warning System. They were our security fences, our motion detectors, and our radars that we might see safely into the night. They flanked us in the field of battle, flushed our food in the hunt, guided and guarded our children. Perhaps most importantly, they give us something our own species seems incapable of—unconditional love.

As for cats, their sensuous grace and sultry beauty earned them a station above toil for keep. As Mark Twain said, "Of all God's creatures, there is only one that cannot be made slave of the lash. That one is a cat." When it suited them, they freed our huts of pestilent rodents. Otherwise they simply observed our daily folly with cool aloofness, and occasionally honored us with their whimsical affection.

Although forged on land, these relationships followed us out upon the Seven Seas. From the frond decks of the Polynesian proas, to the Arabian dhow, to the British Ships of the Line, down to the voyaging yachts of today, everywhere and always, animals have stood steady at our sides. The sea is not frivolous. Out there these animals are not exotic ornaments to our vanity or extensions of our ego. They are hardy comrades, trusted crew, fully sharing the many hardships and rich rewards of the free life afloat.

The close quarters of ship-life creates an intimacy and understanding which leads to love and respect. Bonds are formed, the depth and poignancy of which are only rarely captured in words. I believe Lord Byron did so nearly two hundred years ago when he wrote, "Near this spot are deposited the remains of one who possessed Beauty without Vanity, Strength without Insolence, Courage without Ferocity, and all the Virtures of Man with out his Vices. This Praise, which would be unmean Flattery if inscribed over human ashes, is but a just tribute to the Memory of *Boatswain*, a Dog."

I share these sentiments for I know and love such an animal. Fortunately my words of praise are not yet over her grave, although I dread that day. I once passed five months of soul-sucking solitude through the seemingly unending darkness of an Arctic night. I use the word "passed" for both its meanings, that is "passed" the time, and "passed" the test, the excruciating test of physical and psychological endurance. Although I had no human company, I do not describe having done this "alone", for I had by my side a brave and beautiful kitten named *Halifax*. I, like my ancestors before me, relied upon her honed senses to warn me when the cunning polar bear lay in ambush outside our icebound yacht. But that was the least of her contributions, for I found the beasts outside the boat were not nearly so dangerous as the demons within. When despair dug so deeply into my bones that my own survival seemed of little importance, her survival remained for me a serious responsibility and gave some structure and meaning to my "day". Most importantly, *Halifax* was my friend when I needed one like no other time in my life. Since then we have shared many adventures and, for her, probably too many sea miles. While my wife, Diana, and I frugally hoard our cruising kitty, we do not begrudge a single cent spent on our cruising cat, for her health and welfare remains a primary concern.

While there is a glut of information regarding all other onboard concerns, we have found a paucity of timely and accurate information regarding the care and transportation of animals at sea. Enter Diana Jessie, who brings to this comprehensive and much needed work not only the depth of her 130,000 sea miles and 22 years of live-aboard life, but also her abiding love and respect for animals. Boiled down to its core, her message is that to bring our four-footed friends onboard is not only a joy, but also a responsibility. She meticulously equips us to meet this responsibility with valuable information and advice regarding the selection, care, transportation and importation of shipboard animals. She exudes a heartwarming enthusiasm for her subject, and executes her important duties in an organized, ship-shape and Bristol fashion. *Cruising with Your Four-Footed Friends* deserves a prominent space on every nautical bookshelf. I suggest it be filed under A for animals, that we might see it first and often.

ALVAH SIMON, 2002

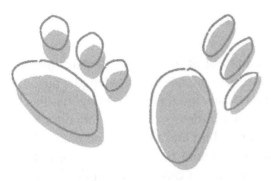

Introduction

Our four-footed friend has traveled more than 30,000 nautical miles and visited Mexico, the Philippines, Japan, Hong Kong, Russia, the Aleutians, Alaska, and Canada. Boca is a neutered black cat adopted from the American Society for the Prevention of Cruelty to Animals, (ASPCA). He took over ownership of our 48-foot sailboat and us at the age of seven weeks. He is not the first cat we've had, and probably will not be the last.

Cruising with Boca has provided us with the opportunity to learn to say "cat" in multiple languages, visit a wide range of veterinary facilities, and personally receive gifts from his new friends. Socially adept from his first day aboard, he has served as an intermediary in making friends in nearly every port we visited. His handsome form sitting like a black statue on the Dorade ventilation box of the main cabin has stopped passers-by in their tracks. His timid character has dissuaded him from wandering, challenging strangers, or taking unnecessary risks. He is a comfortable part of our life as cruisers.

Even before Boca, we realized that many cruisers included cats in their plans. In the last decade, those numbers have increased dramatically. Likewise, the number of cruisers who have dogs on board has increased. At one time, I thought that cats lived on sailboats and dogs lived on powerboats. Wrong! The species varies as much as the breed. Pet size doesn't seem to reflect the size of the vessel either. An Irish setter on a 24-foot sailboat or a tiny toy terrier on an enormous ketch is not exceptional. Friends on a 36-foot sailboat had two large cats while we had one in our 48-foot home.

Some cruisers have birds. Yes, we must admit that they can be companionable and wonderfully entertaining. Unfortunately, they present major problems, especially for those of us who cruise across national borders. Our own agricultural quarantine regulations make it very difficult to take birds in and out of the country. Determining the origin of birds and their exposure to disease involves lengthy quarantine. Birds acquired out of the country are difficult to bring into the country. Additionally, caring for sick birds is extremely difficult and professional care is essential. Taking a bird into a setting and putting it at risk is unacceptable. Just as we admonish responsibility for cats and dogs, we insist on the same for birds. Consequently in this book, we won't address birds due to insufficient information, limited experience, and a shortage of professional expertise.

Exotic animals including ferrets, snakes, and monkeys are great fodder for movies and television programs about cruising. In reality, they are not pets and sometimes dangerous to have aboard. We were tempted to buy a wonderful three-toed sloth while in South America. It seemed friendly and cuddly. However, like so many intriguing animals, we didn't have a clue how to care for it, didn't know where it would live on our boat, and it is not a companion pet. It is a wild animal.

Those without four-footed friends suggest that a goldfish or lizard is a great pet. They just don't understand. We are talking about cruising with companion pets. A common thread within the pet-owning, cruising community is the affection we feel for our animals. Cats and dogs respond to their human friends. Dogs work hard to earn and keep the fondness of their humans. Constant tail-wagging and raised eyebrows communicate the canine desire to please. Cats show restraint but the deep rumbling purrs or the gurgling baby sounds they make as they sit on your newspaper or jump onto your head communicate a bond of affection, after a fashion.

When I first started reading books and articles about pets, I wasn't ready for the references about cat behavior or dog behavior to vary in gender. My cat is a male and articles about cats that used the feminine were disconcerting. However, I didn't expect that people would accept references to all dogs to be masculine. I attempted to solve the problem by using the pronoun "it" when I wasn't writing about a specific pet. The choice of "it" may have been a practical choice, but not thoughtful. As you read, you are likely to note that all cats and dogs have gender, but I tried to give equal time to both genders regardless of the species.

As I researched the topics I thought important to cruisers, I discovered more topics. I interviewed numerous boat owners with pets. Clearly, many people take their pets on their boats for short trips and holidays. Another group of people lives aboard full time and has pets. Moreover, there is the group I originally thought about, the full-time cruisers. According to the Humane Society of the United States, there are more than 73 million cats and 68 million dogs living as companion pets in this country. Those companion pets go with us.

It is my hope and intent to make it easier to enjoy having a pet aboard in a cruising environment. Your boat can be a safe and happy place for all members of the family even the fuzzy ones. If you aren't convinced that your four-footed friend can be happy aboard, this book can help you make an appropriate decision about whether or not to go cruising with your four-footed friends.

Why Do We Take Pets to Sea?

1 Pets seem to be a normal part of many households. In some cases, they are even necessary members of the household. Dogs can assist people that are sight or hearing impaired. The quiet purring of a cat sends messages of contagious contentment. Some pets offer protection for those who feel vulnerable. Research has shown that pets have a soothing and calming effect on distraught children, lonely seniors, and nearly anyone who loves cats and dogs. For many of us, they make themselves necessary and irresistible.

When you decide to go cruising, whether for a summer vacation or the voyage of a lifetime, it is important to contemplate the needs of the family pet. Just because the dog goes everywhere with you doesn't mean it will be comfortable on a boat. Your longhaired cat may have his own frequent flyer account, but that doesn't mean that he is going to be immune to seasickness. The first step then is to recognize what you are doing when you take your dog or cat cruising.

Cutter's Story

"I didn't really want a dog. I didn't want the responsibility," was Nancy's comment as she began to talk about Cutter. Cutter found a home with Art and Nancy White, and he has earned his way. This initial reluctance is not typical of the pet-owning cruisers with whom I spoke.

I begin with Cutter because his owners did not start with an emotional bond for an animal nor were they particularly passionate about dogs. They had cruised without an animal aboard and added Cutter to their family after several years of cruising. Taking on the responsibility of a pet after living on their Valiant 40 makes them more objective than most of the pet owners I encountered.

Cutter is a Schipperke, a Belgian breed of small, stocky, black dogs with a fox-like head and heavy coat. At Art's urging, Cutter joined Art and Nancy at the tender age of six weeks aboard their Valiant 40 *Audrey Lane* when they started on their second trip to Mexico. He traveled with them down the Pacific coast of Mexico and Central America, through the Panama Canal, the Caribbean and finally to Texas, a two-year voyage. Nancy says that she was not enthusiastic about having a dog but today her attitude is quite different.

Cutter, full grown, weighs about 14 pounds. He has dense black fur, a barrel shaped body, short legs, and sharp ears that hear beyond the sea. He is a barge dog bred to live on the barges that ply the canals of Europe. As a choice of dog, he has a head start on many that go cruising. He is small and compact. He does not fear water but is not particularly inclined to play in or around water. Unlike breeds that retrieve and hunt around water, the Schipperke goes in the water to work. When a floating line needs to be retrieved or taken to waiting hands, this black bundle of fur makes short work of the job. He is constantly on the move, watching everything around him. His sense

PHOTOGRAPH BY JESSIE

Cutter, a Schipperke, is a tiny hero with a big heart.

of territory is very highly developed. His capacity to see and hear beyond human capabilities earned him the devotion of his owners.

One day *Audrey Lane* was reaching off the coast of Costa Rica. It was clear, but the waves were huge and there was no visibility between the troughs. Suddenly, Cutter began barking. Art couldn't quiet the dog. Cutter ran forward then returned to Art, all the while barking furiously. Art followed Cutter to the bow, and as the boat crested a wave, he saw a small fishing boat in the trough in their path. He rushed back to the cockpit, changed course, and sailed by an open fishing boat loaded with sleeping fishermen.

On another occasion, Cutter began barking without seeming provocation. Knowing that Cutter barked at sea for cause, Art and Nancy scanned the sea around them. They were passing a large sea buoy and it loomed large. "Cutter knew it was there, and he thought we were too close," explained Nancy. One night he set up a big fuss and they found a family motoring directly into their path in an unlighted boat. Again, Cutter saved them from calamity.

Cutter is a small dog so his owners carry him up the steep companionway ladder. Despite his diminutive size, he has saved his owners from disaster with his great senses and his instinct to alert them. He barks when other boats come alongside but quickly befriends when his owners say "okay." Although many people don't see the appeal in small dogs, this Schipperke has earned his place and his owners' love.

Zorba, the Greek-Cypriot

At the marina in Larnaca, the locals had dumped at least 30 cats and kittens, leaving them homeless. The English cruisers had set up the feeding roster, organizing collecting scraps from the butcher shops and fishmongers. They wailed when the marina management attempted to poison the cats. We rescued one of these furry waifs and our first cruising pet joined us on the island of Cyprus in 1988.

We had already sailed half way around the world when a cruising friend came by our boat one day to say he had rescued three abandoned kittens. He thought he could manage two kittens and wanted the third one to have a home. When my husband told me about the kitten, I was surprised. He sounded interested.

I said, "If I go to see this kitten, you know I will become emotionally involved. Are you ready to have a cat aboard?" Jim just smiled at me and said, "Let's go see the kitten."

The kittens did need a home. It was easy to see why Paul had brought all three of them aboard. They were tiny but their eyes were open and they tumbled over each other with vigor and enthusiasm. Americans are a soft touch when it comes to pets; we are second only to the English in being true "pushovers."

Since we could not be shown up by our English neighbor, we adopted a tiny kitten who quickly made his home in a box of tissues. He was less than five weeks old, and as we were to discover, could fit into the tiniest openings. At a Sunday morning gin fizz party, he crawled into a plastic glass to lick the creamy foam from the edges, and promptly was stuck headfirst in the glass. Everything on our boat must have a purpose. His entertainment value guaranteed he had a home on the boat for life.

Since we were in Greek Cyprus, Zorba seemed the appropriate name for our little feline. He was friendly, energetic, and quickly litter box trained. His favorite game was to stick both forepaws into the hand opening of the various drawers to extract whatever he could reach. Paper products, socks, and dishtowels, were fair game, and our main cabin always looked like a teenager had just passed through. Other than these slovenly habits, he posed no problems. None, that is, until he was big enough to climb the companionway ladder. Even then, we could keep him on board by pulling in the passerelle, the rolling gangway, which prevented him from going ashore. Stern first to the dock, the distance was too great to jump ashore, and the distance to neighbors on either side was too great, for a while.

The first important lesson for Zorba and for us was leash training. It was rare that we were in a marina, but when we were, he would take off at the first opportunity. He wore a harness and leash reluctantly and was always finding a new method for slipping out of it. We were constantly on guard for sudden disappearances. He did like our company and had no objections to riding safely confined in the box on the back of my motor scooter. He normally came when called so we didn't face constant searches.

One day I found him on our bunk with eyes half open, panting and burning up with fever. The swelling made his little black face unrecognizable. An Aussie veterinarian said he would go to the local clinic for some medication but told us to start ice baths immediately as the fever was out of control. We wrapped the cat in towels soaked with ice water. Zorba barely moved. Mike was gone for nearly two hours and when he returned, Zorba had recovered enough that he was resting comfortably, the swelling had receded, and he was lapping up the ice water. The final diagnosis was reaction to a bee sting or spider bite.

Zorba was an accident, not a planned addition, as should be the case when adopting a pet. He was an education and a wonderful experience. When he disappeared from our anchored boat in the middle of the night, we wondered if we would recover from the loss. We didn't look ahead because his absence was painful. It was more than a year before we took the plunge again. This time we planned and we prepared.

We Can't Go Without Him

When I first encountered cruisers with a big dog aboard, I had to ask "why?" The dog was an Irish Setter and the sailboat was 24 feet long. The tall, young couple who owned him admitted space was at a premium. With a smile, they told me that Hershey was part of the family. Room or not, they couldn't go without him. He loved the water and they considered that sufficient reason to take him along.

The couple lived on a very tight budget, just $300 per month. They fished whenever they were at anchor and the rest of their diet consisted of rice, pasta, and oatmeal. They clearly didn't have money for extras and they told me that Hershey ate what they ate.

The dog was in beautiful condition and had an extraordinary disposition. He would swim around the anchorage and bark a greeting as he passed each boat. He would continue to swim around your boat until you waved or called back. No one took him to the shore for walks to relieve himself. He'd swim to shore, do the required activity, and return to the boat. We only heard of one transgression when he failed to return. It was not his fault. The security guards at a resort found him on the beach and assumed he was lost so they fed him and locked him up. His owners found him at the resort after he disappeared and he happily returned with them to the boat with a full stomach. It was easy to understand allowing the dog independence, but the lesson to be learned here: never let your pets go unsupervised.

The most common response when I ask, "Why do you have a pet aboard?" is "We can't go without him/her." Sometimes it is clear to me that the pet is old, and part of the family. Nevertheless, the family can't put off cruising any longer. No one wants to face separation from the family cat or dog on purpose, so the pet goes along. Very often, these owners also make it clear that they do not intend to replace the animal. They are waiting for the pet to die.

Not leaving your cat or dog behind is very laudable but there are instances where it seems like cruelty. We encountered a couple on a boat in Mexico with a St. Bernard. The dog was huge, old, and infirm. The owners took the dog ashore a couple of times daily to defecate and then brought him back to the boat. They never exercised the dog. He lived in the cockpit of a 40' boat. It was clear that the dog was not thriving in this environment. The weather was extremely warm and the sun protection was blue canvas that absorbed the heat. The dog was alone for hours at a time and then they gave him a variety of leftovers and treats to compensate for the lack of attention. The last thing this old, overweight St. Bernard needed was to eat scraps from his owner's dinner plate. Giving food that has sugar and fat isn't a reward for a pet; it can be the cause of a medical problem.

By contrast, we encountered a boat in the Mediterranean that had a three-legged dog aboard. This couple dearly loved the dog and he had traveled everywhere in the world. The dog had some difficulty in getting around but his owners constantly groomed, walked, and gave him loving attention. The dog greeted everyone who came aboard. He was well behaved and rarely barked. He was clearly loved and part of the family. They spared no effort to make him happy and comfortable and to keep him healthy, as it should be.

Dove's Kittens

Robin Lee Graham completed one of the most extraordinary voyages in modern history aboard the 23' foot *Dove*. He is the youngest solo-circumnavigator on record. Unknown to many is that Robin had four-footed friends aboard his small sailboat.

When we talked recently, I asked him if he considers himself an animal person. Now, 32 years after his record-making trip, his response was "We have three cats and seven chickens." He described his life in Montana as being filled with all kinds of animals. "We are looking after a friend's home for awhile and I looked forward to taking care of his five cats, but he took his cats on his trip."

He was 13 on his first sailing trip with his family. They took the family Boston terrier on their trip to the South Pacific. Robin said, "He was a lot of work."

When he prepared for his circumnavigation at age 16, he took two kittens. They had been born in his aunt's closet; Suzette and Joliette set off from Long Beach aboard the boat. When I asked him to recall his preparation for the kittens, he remembered packing kitty litter and cat food aboard. "I didn't have enough and they ate scraps and fish that I caught." He provisioned with canned goods and the kittens enjoyed the canned meat and canned tuna.

Cat litter presented a problem because he ran out of it. He described using sand from the beach, "but the kittens tracked it everywhere." His solution to the problem was ingenious. He took two trays, punched holes in one, and set it into the other tray. He filled it with pea gravel. He didn't have to worry about tracking sand and it was easy for him to clean up the two trays. He rinsed them overboard.

His first two kittens didn't make the whole trip. Susette deserted him for a male cat in the South Pacific. A truck killed Joliette in Fiji. He acquired another kitten that had a feisty attitude and entertained Robin during the long miles. He explained that a flying fish landed on board one day, on his only chart of Darwin. The kitten got to the fish first and tore up the chart in the process. This kitten, Avunga, disappeared from the boat while 10' from a sand quay. He never found him.

Robin finished the last half of his trip with two kittens named Fili and Kili. Fili was blind and Kili had poor vision. The two kittens managed very well aboard despite their disabilities. Fili gave birth to four kittens, two of them survived, Piglet and Pooh. Although Fili had been lost overboard, when Robin reached his starting point in Long Beach, he still had Kili, Pooh, and Piglet aboard. In his last year of cruising, he said of the cats, ". . . a nuisance sometimes, but it was great to have them. Just seeing something alive helped."

Kili lived another ten years with Robin and Patti, his wife, in the mountains of Montana. Now his favorite cat, like most of the kittens that sailed with him, is orange. This cat, named Kato, offers the same dimension to his life as the little four-footed sailors who helped him sail around the world. "They gave me companionship when I really needed it."

One of the primary lessons we need to learn is vigilance. Pets are dependent on humans and when you adopt one you are responsible for that animal's life. Losing a pet at sea or on land is devastating.

Boris, the Handsome

When I asked Ann McDougall why she took her Giant Schnauzer cruising, she told me, "Boris is a great friend and I need his companionship." As we talked about Boris, it was like a tennis match as he looked at me and then looked at Ann. Every time he looked at Ann his bushy black eyebrows went up as if to say, "Yes, what do you think of me?" Moreover, with each answer, he seemed to nod approval. Before the interview was over, he couldn't stand watching us and finally moved close to Ann so she could put her arm over his shoulders.

She stopped and commented that this was really why she was glad to have Boris along because he was so comforting. For many cruisers—maybe more for women but men sense it also—when a situation is stressful, the undemanding attention of an animal communicates comfort and faith. This reassurance encourages us to cope with whatever fear or frustration is at hand. I could feel that comfort emanating from Boris.

Meet Halifax

I received a letter from a good cruising friend, Mary Iverson. She sent a letter about their encounter with another cruiser . . . always a source of great stories.

Mary's story was that she'd met a person in Auckland named Alvah. Nice guy, the hour she knew him. They talked about pets on board.

He was going to pick up his cat from 30-day quarantine the next day. He said he owed his life to his cat and as far as he was concerned, whatever that cat wanted, she got. Whatever it took to keep her well, he would do. His story was about a time he and his wife were in the Arctic. One month into the winter, his wife had to be air evacuated out for a family emergency. He and this new kitten were left alone for almost five months. He was not yet a converted "cat person." Periodically he would open up the boat to let the cat go out to do her business or for them to go stretch their legs, fish, whatever. Normally the cat would gladly take a break from the confines of the boat. Well, one time the hatch was opened to let the cat take her break but she wouldn't go out! Okay, so she's lazy or it's too cold, or whatever. Later that day, Alvah went out and there were polar bear prints everywhere! From that day on, for the rest of their time alone, he'd open the hatch, encourage his little furry buddy to go out and any hesitation, neither one would go. Almost every time, when they finally did go out, he'd find some danger had been in the area. He was convinced the cat is the only reason he got out of there alive. Most likely he's right. Clearly, Alvah now LOVES his cat!

What Mary didn't know was Alvah Simon had written a great book about their Arctic adventure, *North to the Night*, in which the kitten, Halifax, had played an important role. I will tell you more about their adventure in chapter five.

The Boys on *Charbonneau*

Max and Bailey, a pair of handsome golden retrievers, cruise with Blaine and Janet Parks aboard S/V *Charbonneau* in the Caribbean. The dogs are charmers, and they open many doors for Blaine and Janet as they travel. Janet explained that young children love the dogs and insist on holding the leash. The dogs are quite an attraction and Janet and Blaine have to exercise caution with their new, young, exuberant friends. It is hard to go unnoticed when your arrival with two dogs initiates a mini-parade involving the children of the town.

Although those who don't have pets aboard see traveling with pets as onerous, there is a big payback for those who persevere. Strangers often find it hard to talk to one another. This is especially true in

PHOTOGRAPH BY BLAINE PARKS

Bailey and Max are popular with all children.

foreign countries. The presence of pets, just like the presence of small children, creates a climate that makes communication possible. It gives us something in common. We are social creatures and our shared affection for pets creates the common ground we need. The joy of cruising is knowing the country and its people. Pets help make it possible to have that experience. Janet and Blaine are twice as lucky.

Tarzoon, the Jungle Buffoon

Tania Aebi is the youngest woman to circumnavigate single-handed. Her feline companion for the last half of her amazing voyage was a kitten from Vanuatu. These are her words:

"The story of Tarzoon's life away from the nest begins in my arms and on my lap in the self-contained world of my boat in the South Pacific. Together, from the island of Efate in the Vanuatu group where I picked him out of a litter of kittens, we sailed on toward endless horizons, through storms and calms, anchoring in harbors with land only accessible by a dinghy. Until New York, where he stepped ashore for good, without looking back, the boat was virtually all he knew about the world. Perhaps it is because he spent the first eighteen months of life on a twenty-six-foot sailboat with a seven-and-a-half foot beam that he never became a very large cat, but what he lacks in size he has made up for with experience and character."

We live a finite amount of time and the window of opportunity for cruising is often very small. I don't believe that your pet should determine your plans, but if the pet is part of the plan, give that cat or dog due consideration. Before assuming you cannot go without your pet, think about what consequences she will endure. If it is a large dog, do you have enough space, can you supply sufficient exercise, is the breed one that can survive the weather? Have you made trial trips with your pet to see how he reacts? Just because you love your pet and you love cruising, it does not mean your pet will love cruising.

What is the Best Seagoing Pet?

2 Finding the best pet for cruising is simple. It is the one you have when you go. That is a roundabout way of admitting that most people don't plan on the kind of pet they will take cruising. They make the decision to go and then they decide if they want to take their pet along. Determining whether or not your pet will enjoy the trip should be part of your decision.

Basic to your enjoyment of cruising and the happiness of your pet is the necessity that your dog or cat is spayed or neutered before you go. Especially for long term cruising, having a female in heat or a male on the prowl will make your life miserable. Spraying and marking will make your boat and the surrounding area uninhabitable. Trying to clean up those smells or live with them in a small area is intolerable. You will not be welcome in a fleet of cruisers with a sexually active cat or dog. In chapter seven, we address the issues of pet etiquette and expectations.

There are some health benefits for your spayed or neutered pet. Research has shown that in dogs spayed six months or earlier, it helps to prevent breast cancer.

Overnights, Holidays, and Summer Vacations

Taking your dog or cat aboard for a night or weekend is a common practice and treated very casually. Some pets have difficulty with a change in environment, even if it is only temporary. Just as some humans don't adjust to boats, some pets don't adjust to boats either. The two solutions for humans in making the adjustment to boat life are time or medication; the resolution is the same for pets.

If your cat or dog is nervous, frightened, or physically upset by being on the boat, give him some time. Your pet probably has learned about riding in a car. The car may represent happy outings or it may represent unpleasant trips to the veterinarian. If you want your pet to adapt to cruising then you want the experiences to be happy. Going to the boat should be fun for everyone. You will need to allow time for this.

Before going anywhere on the boat, your pet needs to have some time to become acquainted and adapt to the boat. Think about your pet's perspective. Knowing that sudden noises or movements scare your pet or that she is very nervous about water will sensitize you to the problems you might encounter. If you have a powerboat, take your pet to the boat to familiarize her with new surroundings and obstacles. Don't power up the engines on the pet's first couple of visits. Just let him wander about and get comfortable. Dogs and cats will sniff everything until they are satisfied. Don't rush this first process. A big boat may take some time so let your buddy become acquainted with the area. If you were moving to a new home, you would go through the same process.

Let your pet understand that a boat will be a floating house. Have a meal aboard and let your pet see how you behave. Offer her water in a location you plan to use regularly for feeding. Talk to your pet, reassure him, and make him feel welcome. If your animal is comfortable, a nap will be the first indicator. Let your pet snooze and then take him home. If he becomes comfortable and then you interrupt this adjustment, your pet may conclude that he is not expected to be comfortable or nap on the boat. Make several return visits to the boat fairly soon. You don't want your pet to forget what the boat is like and have to start over again. You want to reaffirm that the boat is a second home and a safe, comfortable place for your pet.

Take a brief ride on your boat after your animal has become acquainted. Dogs and cats have very sensitive hearing. When you fire up the engines, make sure your pet is away from the engine room or engine box. If there are enough people on board the boat to spare one from the necessary operations of leaving the dock, have someone stay with your pet to reassure her that the noise and movement are okay. The forward part of the boat is generally quieter because you are away from the exhaust and the noise. Never let your pet roam in the engine room whether the engine is on or not. Many chemicals could seriously harm your cat or dog. Keep chemical containers closed and the outsides clean if you store them somewhere your pet can get into. Remember that cats and small dogs can get into small spaces in your boat. They can find places from which they may not be easily retrieved. Places that you may not even know about.

Powerboats typically have larger engines than sailboats, but any engine can startle your cat or dog. Remember this the first time you decide to take a dinghy ride. Keep your pet in a secure place when turning on the engine. Small dogs feel much more secure if you hold them. Large dogs and cats should be close by so that you can pet them, hold the leash, and talk softly to them. The sound will cause a reaction, but you can help your pet recover quickly.

Typically, sailboats don't have as loud or powerful an engine as a powerboat. However, be considerate of your pet when starting the motor. There are other noises on sailboats to which cats can be extremely sensitive. Tacking and jibing involves noise both on deck and below deck. We have watched Boca through 30,000 miles and discovered that straightforward noise below is annoying. However, on deck the noise in concert with watching huge white things flapping in the air is frightening. He will be sound asleep on deck and the noise from a momentary luff will wake him. If it continues, he disappears below at warp speed. His predecessor had no such fear. In fact, we had to make him stay below when we thought conditions were too rough. Watch your cat closely when trimming sails. If he is frightened, make sure he stays below. A sudden fright might cause your cat to jump the wrong direction. A leash and harness or a personal flotation device (PFD) can keep this from becoming a tragedy.

Motion sickness is caused by our sensory system being out of sync with what we expect. Our senses have taught us that land is still and that curbs and ladders don't move. Your pet expects his world to be just as stationary. The motion of a boat defies everything our senses have communicated. Allow time for adjustment of the senses. Dogs will stay in the cockpit underway to be with you. Cats are more likely to go below and burrow into a bunk or hide in a locker. Regardless of how your pet reacts, give her time to become comfortable. Avoid big seas and fast turns. Let your pet try to overcome the new sensations in her own way and on her own schedule.

If your pet has problems with the motion of the boat, check with your veterinarian about medication for seasickness. We have found that pets generally respond as humans; they go to sleep. If your trip is going to be overnight or a few days, you may want to rethink your plans. You might be happier and your pet more comfortable if you just get a sitter or kennel your dog or cat. Remember all members of your family, including the fuzzy ones, are supposed to have fun.

The Best Sailors

Cat owners think a cat is the best sailor. Dog owners believe that a dog is the best shipmate. Robin Graham was very candid. "I wouldn't take a dog. I think they are a lot of work. I am a cat person. I like having cats around." Our choices depend on our experiences, both good and bad with cats and dogs. We are influenced by the kind of pet we have when we go cruising or the kind of pet we want.

We have mentioned our cruising friends in the Mediterranean who had an old, three-legged pooch that could barely manage life on a boat. They made all kinds of adaptations and adjustments in their cruising style and schedule to accommodate the dog. They built an elaborate gangway for boarding. They provided a special diet. They made stops so the dog could have short walks; not convenient for them, but necessary for the dog. He had been their companion for many years and they could not imagine living without him. The dog, despite disabilities and ailments, enjoyed the cruising and barked happily at birds, liked fishing boats, and loved meeting new people. In spite of all of his difficulties, this dog's life was a happy one. It was a sad day when we heard the dog had died of old age.

Canadian friends bought and refurbished an old steel powerboat and went cruising in Mexico. They had two house cats that were destined to travel with them. The cats had never been on board, had never lived outdoors, and had experienced very little variety in their environment. At middle age, the cats were brought aboard. According to Susan, the cats stayed below in the forward stateroom and slept. They came up to the galley to eat, to the head for the litter box, and then would go back to bed. Finally, one of the cats ventured out of a companionway to look around the anchored boat. He explored and

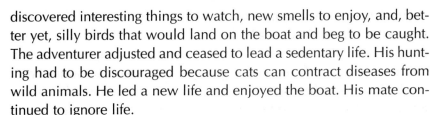

discovered interesting things to watch, new smells to enjoy, and, better yet, silly birds that would land on the boat and beg to be caught. The adventurer adjusted and ceased to lead a sedentary life. His hunting had to be discouraged because cats can contract diseases from wild animals. He led a new life and enjoyed the boat. His mate continued to ignore life.

Years ago, my vote would have gone to cats as the best sailors. The reason was there were more of them in the long distance cruising community. However, over the years we have seen many dogs and cats living happily on board. The owner is the person who makes cruising with a cat or a dog the right choice.

Water Babies

People who grow up in the desert, the mountains, or near the water each have different experiences and therefore a different perspective on their surrounding. Their environment is part of their background. Animal breeds are similar because they develop to live and work in specific surroundings. Having said that you're thinking, "Cats hate water." Cats have that reputation but it isn't entirely accurate. The species developed in the desert where it ate snakes and green plants. However, since that time, the species has developed to fit in whatever the environment. Siberian tigers rolling in the snow or Bengal tigers playing king-of-the-mountain in a rocky stream are proof of felines finding ways of enjoying their surroundings. Felines enjoy water, as anything else, when they are in control. One breed of cat, the Turkish Van, is often called the "swimming cat." This medium, longhair cat is typically white with piebald markings and has a plumy tail. The coat has the texture of cashmere and there is no undercoat. This cat evolved in the Middle East where the weather has extremes of heat and cold. He is very adaptable to temperature changes. The Van can and does swim underwater to catch fish.

Most cats will sit and watch water, play with the stream of water from the tap, drink from the toilet, and a few actually get into water to swim and play. We had one water cat that was so enthusiastic about chasing birds that after a half-hour of stalking, he jumped out of our dinghy to catch a duck. Foxy had failed to recognize that although the duck was in the water, it could escape by flying away. Foxy didn't seemed surprised by the water, but rather the fact that the duck flew away. The fact that ducks float better than cats was also a nasty shock. Our unsuccessful, damp, and slightly embarrassed cat, swam back, climbed up the outboard, back into the dinghy, and ignored our amusement.

There are some cats and dogs bred to be in the water or near it. If however someone asked me whether I would take a Golden Retriever or a Schipperke cruising, I would choose the latter. Both dogs are bred to water and working around water. Clearly, retrievers enjoy water and watching them frolic and play in or near the water is great entertainment. The Schipperke doesn't necessarily enjoy being in the water. Nevertheless, she knows water and how to live and work with it. Furthermore, the retriever grows to a large size with large requirements while a Schipperke remains about the size of a retriever puppy. The Portuguese Water Dog and the Dutch Keeshond, somewhat larger than a Schipperke, are also bred for a boating environment.

Most dogs will swim without much encouragement. All dogs need exercise and this is one of the easiest ways for big dogs on boats to get their daily romp. Dogs need to be monitored when they swim, but being in the water retrieving or playing with people is fun for all participants. If you are not prepared to supervise the swimming of your dog, don't encourage him to swim. If you can't get your dog out of the water in an emergency (see Chapter 11) or provide mouth-to-nose resuscitation (see Chapter 10), do not permit your dog to swim from your boat.

Big or Small?

The size of an adult animal should influence your choice of cruising pet. All puppies and kittens are cute. It is their job. Nevertheless, a cute baby can grow into a large problem if you are unprepared. For the short term, a large animal can survive without lots of space for eating or sleeping. Your German Shepherd or mastiff will forgive you for an uncomfortable night or two more readily than she will forgive being left behind.

You need to think seriously about these questions. Can you lift and carry your full-grown pet? Even if he is wet? Carrying sufficient food or water to take care of a weekend or week's vacation isn't a problem. On the other hand, a three-week passage with a 120-pound German Shepherd on your 30-foot cruiser could be debilitating for you and the dog.

Rarely is the size of a cat an issue on a boat. However, I think in terms of a large cat because its chances for survival are better. Having read about Simon's Halifax, clearly kittens are tough. Over the long term, a large adult cat may have a better chance of surviving being in the water but this is speculation on my part. To prove that small may mean better, this is the story of Polar the Wonder Cat and his first overboard experience on an Express 37 sailed by Adam Loory and Jenni Rodda as told by Jenni.

"Polar went overboard while we were moored in the harbor in Jamestown, Rhode Island. It was a very quiet evening, and Polar was out for his evening's constitutional—a run around the boat, up through the stern ports, all along the deck, down the forward hatch, all through the salon, and back out the stern ports, a loop like a running track. Given the downward slope of our transom, this route made for a good run, with a little uphill exercise—until Polar decided to reverse his course: on his first loop in the wrong direction, he slid off the transom at full speed, missed the stern ports, and ended up in the water, PLOP. Adam went over the transom

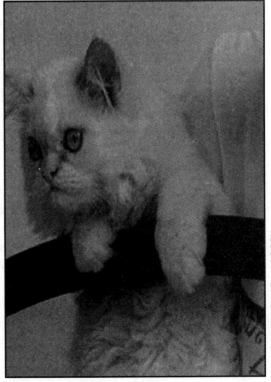

Polar the Wonder Cat is small but fearless and resilient.

on the boarding ladder, and I walked along the toerail, each of us calling to him; we were afraid he'd be caught underneath the boat as it bounced and swung at the stern. Polar swam towards each of us in turn, doing a good job of keeping his head dry, his very long fur streaming out behind him like seaweed. He finally swam close enough to Adam at the stern that Adam was able to stick his foot out for Polar to grab—which he did, full claws out, hanging on for dear life. Watching Adam come up the ladder one-footed, with a very wet, very unhappy cat hanging on to his foot, was something I wished I'd had a camera for! We rinsed Polar off in fresh water, toweled him off, and then left him to his toilette. His distaste for salt water showed on his face with every lick to his fur. Seeing our usually very fluffy, longhaired cat completely wet reminded us just what a little guy he is; there's very little cat (only about 7 pounds worth, even now) underneath all that fur. While none the worse for his swim, Polar did decide that he wanted to be someplace where he felt warm and safe that night; he took up a spot in the V-berth with us, curled up against Adam's tummy. And we closed the stern ports."

The Express has opening ports in the transom, if you are not familiar with the design.

If you have a purebred animal, predicting the adult size is simple. The breeders control the parameters of any breed. They know exactly the size range in terms of weight and height. Generally, they know most of the habits of their breed. The only down side with purebreds comes from the genetic control. Inbreeding perpetuates all characteristics, good or bad.

The mixed-breed pet may tax your imagination. The combination of characteristics is predictable if you know the breed of the parents. We have never known the parents of any of our pets. However, they have proved to be happy, endearing, and smart. If you want a pet but aren't sure what is best, visit the local shelters and pet adoption groups. The perfect dog or cat will tell you if you are the perfect person.

If you spend the time acclimatizing your pet to your boat, you will soon discover whether you can live with his size. Moreover, during the adjustment period, keep in mind the quantity of food you will need to cover a long trip, determine the specific space for sleeping and eating, and where the animal will eliminate. The difference in accommodations for humans on a 25-foot boat and a 50-foot boat are substantial. The difference is substantial for your pet.

Sidney, a large Golden Retriever, cruises with Murray, a mixed terrier, on a large trawler. Murray has no problem negotiating the passageways, steps, and boarding. His "big brother" is comfortable but he does have problems. He doesn't like to step over the twelve-inch space between the dock and the boat. He is a full-grown dog and sometimes has to go to the end of a passageway to turn around, as there isn't enough space for a four-footed U-turn. Sidney has found a way to overcome the handicap of his size and clearly enjoys cruising.

Narrow passageways can present problems for big dogs.

PHOTOGRAPH BY JESSIE

Tyler, a large German Shepherd is agile despite his 120-pound body. Nevertheless, he is very cautious walking around in the cockpit and on deck. His own senses make him aware of the narrow paw spaces and the deck curvature. As he ages, the problems may increase as many large dogs have hip problems causing their hind legs to be less mobile.

If you are saying to yourself, "I can live with the small space," don't forget that your pet has to live with it too. Think about what is fair for both of you.

Cat or Dog?

Deciding whether to take a cat or dog cruising is first a matter of which species you prefer. Only you can make that determination. If your children are involved in the cruising, you may want their input when you consider the pros and cons that might influence your decision. Is your pet to be their companion? Will the children be responsible for upkeep and feeding? Will a pet and children be too much of a distraction in an emergency on the boat? Deciding to take both a cat and a dog to keep peace in the family requires serious soul searching.

Dogs are responsive and demonstrative. They are social creatures just as we are. They seem to sense and respond to your feelings. Generally, they are easily trained because they want to please you and make you happy. At the same time, dogs are often frightening to strangers. As a pet owner, you might feel more secure knowing that your dog is frightening. A barking or growling dog can be a serious deterrent to strangers who might think about boarding your boat. Dogs can be trained not to wander or prowl while their feline counterpart is usually restrained. The relationship with a human makes the dog dependent, and at the same time, dependable.

A young man who was born to cruising parents and has spent his whole life cruising sent a letter to me about having a dog on board.

" I've lived all my life without a family dog but I've always been in contact with them. When I was young, I thought I was good with dogs (what kid doesn't?). Then life went on and I gave away all my toys, play guns, and recently most of my precious buddies (stuffed animals). There was no better time for me to find a dog. I was feeling the empty space between childhood and adolescence.

"Dad found Ilia in a nice little water front house in Ilia Mozambique living with a pleasant Finnish retired Aid worker, now self employed. Ilia had a family of seven dogs (all Jack Russell's) including her mother and her brother from another litter. We received Ilia when she was 7 weeks old and brought her into our home and family.

"At this point, I would like to describe our cockpit. It is located in the center of the boat and has two levels one for sitting on and the other for your feet (where the drainage holes are). The second layer at that time in Ilia's life was too tall for her to climb out. As a result, we used the bottom layer as a cage without the bars.

"I made a cardboard/plastic box house (which she destroyed trying to get out to see us) and a plastic vegetable container with three-quarters of the open part covered by cardboard all equipped with blankets and cushions. In short, she lived like a queen.

"The bottom of the cockpit was her domain for about a month. She had her bed, water, food, hunting territory if you will, and pee/poop paper (which within a few days changed into a rug, which we later dragged over board when it becomes soiled). She was content, safe, and secure.

"If you are bringing up a dog or are thinking about getting one I would suggest you do intentionally what we did by chance (that being putting her inside a controlled environment, like the lower part of the cockpit).

"We sailed from Ilia Mozambique (were we got the dog, fitting isn't it?) to Bazaruto where she had her first encounter with water, real beaches and walks around islands. One time we walked around the island of Santa Carolina and toward the end of our exhausting trek she had had enough. So I very easily put her in a basket under my shoulder, and she slept the rest of the way. It amazes me how Ilia can sleep anywhere.

"From there we came to Richards Bay, South Africa where we still are now.

"I would like to express the psychological side of having a dog in two parts the first part label BD and the second, DD.

"Basic psychology: the grass is always greener on the other side. BD, or before dog, I always wanted a dog, although after I thought about the realities for a while I didn't want to clean up after it, walk, bathe, and be harsh to it when the dog deserved it. At that time, the work of caring for an animal was too overpowering for me. So we did not get a dog by normal means e.g. going to the pound or looking in the paper.

"Instead, we found our puppy by chance. (They were going to sacrifice her in a pagan ritual as she has one blue and one brown eye.)

"BD, I wasn't a very kid oriented person; I preferred adult conversations and debates. At that time, I liked grown-ups better because they did not gang up, tease, and challenge as many children do. Also I was too eager to grow up (I hadn't read Peter Pan yet) and be respected by grown ups although (in my mind) I was already as experienced, well

A small dog like this Jack Russell is his owner's best friend.

spoken (I mean vocabulary not speech, I had a small stutter) and as learned as some of them. But after BD was over and the second phase began, I too started a new chapter in my life, DD-during dog.

"I was for once able to play with a living creature that had the same amount of energy as I. I was able to play free from worry of teasing and tension. Able to play, as any kid should be allowed to do. I now have a best friend that I didn't have to sail away from when the boat moved on.

"Now that we are again in society, I find the magic of a longstanding friend to be holding out against all the sieges of social torment. I feel that if a person is lonely or wishing for something more, something much greater than him or herself, that person need not look too far. For a friend will be found in every loved dog, one that will not tease and cause anger, only one that will help when help is needed and love throughout it's entire life.

"Although boats are different, we feed Ilia the same way many other people do, with dog pellets, table scraps, bones, and the odd fishtail if we can catch one!

"She now sleeps either on the couch, my bed, my parent's bed, or in her own bed, which she loves dearly. I am very glad that we have a Jack Russell, even though they are renowned for their hyperactivity, in no way do they (at least Ilia doesn't) need the same amount of exercise. If we play for about 10 minutes 5 times a day with 'rat' (an old sock) and take her for two big walks and maybe one small one she'll be content. When we are sailing, Ilia is at her peak of happiness, prancing up and down the deck like Captain Bligh, she even loves being at sea more than at anchor. A born sailor if I say so myself, never gotten sea sick even once.

"I wish you could see Ilia's little head peeking over the coaming as we row about in the dinghy, grinning in utter happiness. I truly believe that dogs are one of man's best friends. And that a boat is a dog's dream come true.

From,

Falcon Riley. Age 14

The single, biggest disadvantage for a dog on a boat is lack of agility. The body structure does not allow it to be nimble. Blunt toenails don't dig in and hang on the way feline claws can. The cat can climb and hang on or burrow into a small space while you must provide a dog with a protected space for rough times at sea. A dog must have a safe place particularly if you need to steer, trim sails, or make repairs in bad weather. If a dog gets excited or frightened while you are trying to accomplish a task, you can hardly spend your time reassuring your dog. A panicked dog at your heels is not useful in an emergency.

Other issues that deter some cruisers from taking a dog are how to handle exercise, groom your pet, and how to manage toilet habits. We will discuss these issues more completely later in the book.

Cats appear to be less responsive than dogs but that impression might change when you live in the confines of a boat. The independent style of a cat, and the fact that he doesn't appear to need human approval is one reason that people take cats cruising. Likewise, we assume the cat is a useful animal because mice and rats are common in the waterfront environment. Stalking wild rodents may seem natural, but as indicated before, wild life can pass on disease and pests. Hunting should be limited to catnip creatures and treats. Exercise is an issue for most cats but life aboard doesn't prevent them from all the typical cat activities. Most cats are easily trained to a litter box. Many people believe that cats can exist on a diet of fish, so they assume diet is not a problem.

A cat is physically able to manage rough rides. His innate sense to climb up and to hang on with his claws permits him to avoid falls and injury. When the cat recognizes he is at risk, he will find a secure spot. On the boat in bad weather that spot is usually low and close to the center of the boat. A cat senses danger when he isn't in control. When in danger, our cat appears to go into hibernation; he neither eats nor drinks and doesn't use the litter box. Only once have we had our cat seek us out during rough weather. Typically, he burrows under gear or into a locker.

Polar the Wonder cat finds his niche behind the center companionway, behind the engine and battery box, close to the centerline, just back of the keel. He has to get very flat, and scrunch himself down underneath the ice chest to work his way back there. Jenni said, "We've 'lost' him there more than once, since he's also hard to see once he gets comfy!"

If the rough seas last for several days, make a point of finding your cat and checking on her health; too long without food or water is not good for her. Unless she is sick, she will find water and food as needed. When the weather subsides, cats typically resume their normal routine.

Leaving cats to fend for themselves on the boat for a day or two is a common practice. If they have sufficient food, water, and litter, they will only scold you slightly upon return. Dogs don't like to be alone, and they pine and fret when you leave them. Dogs are frenetic when you return, suddenly reassured that you still love them. Cats will recognize your return but after a civilized rub or pat, return to detached independence. Frequently, cruisers want to take an excursion from the boat but pets limit those opportunities. A trip of several days to sightsee in a historic city or trek through the jungle may not be practical with a pet. Even taking your pet to a local restaurant may be a problem, particularly in countries where his cousins may be on the menu. Think about your pet in terms of how she will be included in your off-the-boat activities as well as when you are at anchor or underway.

Some cruisers have multiple pets. Our marina neighbors have two dogs and another couple, on the next dock, has two cats. Sometimes the circumstances of pet ownership aren't planned, and you find yourself with multiple pets because you love animals. At other times, people intentionally choose to have two pets. We have spoken with several cruisers who have a pair of cats because they keep each other company.

Some assumptions about cats might create the impression that cats need to have a playmate. I think many people assume that cats are independent and will associate only with other cats. Others feel a bit of guilt about leaving cats alone for long periods so they get two cats to overcome this feeling. Cats are loners by choice. They can get along with other cats, but unlike dogs, they don't have a pack mentality.

From my point of view, the best justification for two pets is because you enjoy their company and want them aboard. Max and Bailey are retrievers cruising aboard a sailboat in the Caribbean. They are inseparable from each other and their owners. In fact, the four of them constitute a family. The two dogs are family members and are given that kind of consideration.

Maggi and Bubba are young Burmese cats. Weighing in at seven pounds each, together they aren't any bigger than our cat. They have unique personalities, they are clearly identifiable, and they are a constant source of pleasure for their owners. Their antics are always entertaining but their charm is clear whether they are sleeping wrapped up in each other,

Two pets may be double the fun, but they are double the responsibility as well.

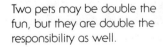

PHOTOGRAPH BY JESSIE

fighting over the same toy, or sharing their scratching post. Pets can be taught to share and live together.

Making a commitment to two pets is not a simple doubling of effort or a simple solution to a perceived problem. Make sure your pets are compatible with each other before you put them in a new environment.

Personality

Experience with cats and dogs shows that their personalities can be as varied as that of humans. Trying to make sure that your pet will have a personality suited to cruising and suited to you is important. There is a trait that we share with cats and dogs that makes a substantial difference in personality development. It is confidence. The kitten or puppy that is confident has some identifiable characteristics at an early age. Normally, the characteristics stay with them into adulthood.

PHOTOGRAPH BY JESSIE

A puppy with attitude will become a confident adult with personality.

PHOTOGRAPH BY JESSIE

A kitten with curiosity and attentiveness reflects the personalities of her parents.

Look for the kitten that carries his tail erect. Look for curiosity so important to a cat. She will sniff and search without fear. Look for attentive behavior and responsiveness to toys, catnip, and quick motion. We think in terms of the mother cat nurturing and protecting her kittens and look to her for future patterns in her kittens. However, the ten seconds of desire from the now absent Tom is the other half of the imprint the kitten demonstrates. You need to spend time with the kitten before making a final selection.

Look for the puppy that comes forward, demands attention, and is frolicsome and playful. This confident puppy grows into a confident and dependable companion. The winsome little puppy that is shy and timid may be hard pressed to be brave. She may become the dog without confidence, the one that is fearful, that will bark all night, nip at people, and be driven to an uncontrolled frenzy. The fearful dog will not be a good cruising companion.

Breeds

Fear and aggression are a dangerous combination. Some breeds should be avoided because the fearful dog from an aggressive breed is often a menacing dog. There are some breeds to avoid because they are banned from entry into certain countries. An example is this list of dogs not accepted into various Pacific Rim Countries:

- dogo Argentino;
- fila Brazileiro;
- Japanese tosa;
- Pit bull (includes the American pit bull terrier, the American bulldog, Staffordshire bull terrier, and crosses between them and other breeds);
- Neapolitan Mastiff
- Akita

Other breeds that may present a risk are the Chow, Sharpie, Rottweiler, and the Queensland heeler. In public places the Bull Mastiff, Bull Terrier, Doberman, German Shepherd and the related breeds such as the Belgian Shepherd and East European Shepherd, Rottweiler and Presa Canario may be required to be muzzled.

Cats and dogs that are mixes with wild animals may not be acceptable unless you can prove they are at least five generations from the wild parent. Wild animals should not be kept as pets. Knowing you have a potential problem with your pet, prepare yourself to manage the situation.

Fawna

We have to share a very special pet at this point. Fawna is a toy fox terrier. She is the third of that breed that Mike Ganahl and Leslie Hardy have had as a cruising companion. She is eight and a half years old and weighs three pounds. She eats four ounces of canned dog food daily. She doesn't drink water because she gets sufficient moisture from her food. Her size and the small amount of food she digests make a plastic tray about 10x18 inches lined with a paper towel sufficient as her litter box. When things are rough, she sleeps in a small

Fawna takes up very little space and gives back tons of affection.

carry bag tightly lodged in a cubby. She has a separate bag for travel that can be zipped closed. She is well behaved and her diminutive size makes it possible for her to travel anywhere. Her owners had to search to find a tiny PFD but she wears it easily.

Unlike many small dogs that are typically nervous and noisy, Fawna is quiet, well behaved, and very affectionate. Like most dogs, she loves attention, cuddling, and staying close to her humans. In addition to her various bags, PFD, and litter pan, she also sports a lovely collection of necklaces. Leslie shares bead bracelets and other jewelry with Fawna. We don't advocate dressing pets, but Fawna's constant presence allows her to be monitored and accidents avoided.

Boat life agrees with Fawna. She likes the routine. Mike pointed out that she is happiest with a routine and least happy when her routine is upset.

When and How Do I Start?

3 Ideal situations are a result of planning. If you decide to take a dog or a cat cruising, there are ways to give yourself a head start. We've talked about advantages and disadvantages in having a pet aboard. Now it is important to look at how you can accommodate your pet aboard your boat.

Boarding

One couple we read about said that they selected their boat based on cruising with two dogs, a Labrador Retriever, and a Norwegian Elkhound. On first reading that may sound extreme, but if you are serious cruisers and have large pets, it makes excellent sense. Both of these dogs grow to be large. Carrying either one of the dogs for more than a few minutes could prove to be difficult. Therefore, boarding a boat needs to be considered.

When you take your pet down to the dock, can he climb onto your boat without effort? It is easy to carry cats and small dogs aboard your boat. Large breed dogs are different. They are not always eager to step or jump onto a floating object. A short plank if the incline is not steep is a quick answer. If the seas are rough, or your big pooch is not as sure footed as he was as a puppy, a safety net under the plank may also save everyone an unexpected swim.

A boat with a solid bulwark should have an opening to permit you and your dog to walk through. How high that bulwark is above the dock or the water can be a serious problem for your dog. Some bulwarks have small steps affixed for climbing over, but they may not be adequate for a dog to negotiate. If you have a solid bulwark without a door, then dock steps and a short plank will allow the dog to climb onto the boat.

Sailboats are constructed so that the topsides are at least a foot or so above the water. On large cruising sailboats, the freeboard may rise four or five feet above the water. This requires negotiating a set of steps and gangway or learning to jump from the dock. Again, jumping over an unknown open space on to a moving target is not always an easy skill for a dog to learn.

We were in Iwakuni, Japan, and weather made it necessary to find shelter. There was a United States Marine Corp Air Station with United States Navy support teams at Iwakuni. The navy was happy to help us tie up and avoid the weather. However, the USMC had to send over a security contingent with a customs officer to inspect the boat. The group included a large German Shepherd "sniffer" dog that was to board and inspect the boat. The dock where we tied and the rail of the boat were at the same height, but there was a gap of about 18 inches in between. The dog did not want to cross that open space over the water. The dog's unwillingness to board our boat embarrassed the sergeant who was the handler. Ultimately, the dog had to be lifted aboard by the sergeant. After touring the deck, the dog was confronted with a steep ladder to access below decks. He scrambled down the ladder landing in a heap at the bottom. When the dog finished below, he found climbing back up the ladder was easier. Then the pair attempted to disembark. Just as a dog will unknowingly entangle himself and his leash in a chair, this dog had difficulty with the lifelines on our boat. The sergeant using the lifeline gate and the dog leaping between lifelines complicated leaving the boat. The leash was wrapped in the lifelines leaving the dog suspended. My husband and the sergeant finally extracted a very anxious and unhappy dog. After this ordeal, the sergeant explained that the dog had never been required to board a sailboat. Most of his sniffing was confined to airplane cargo holds and the occasional passenger plane.

Once aboard the boat, there is another access issue as described above, getting below. With powerboats, the configuration is more often kinder to a dog. The water level deck is generally the main living area where your pet will spend most of her time. Climbing to an upper deck or a fly bridge can be difficult, the downward trip is usually worse. You may want to consider keeping your dog below or rigging some other method of climbing to higher decks. If there is

This customized ramp makes access easy for a big dog.

enough room, a ramp with a shallow incline can allow your dog access to the upper decks. Multilevel powerboats such as our neighbor's Nordhaven are definitely dog friendly.

Sailboats generally have a ladder to get to shelter below decks. Two or three-step ladders are usually easy for a dog to negotiate. However, the larger boats with ladders of four or five-step, present a serious challenge for some dogs. Tristan is a young, 65-pound standard poodle living on a big sailboat. He is agile and has no problems climbing. He has been a boat dog since puppyhood and does not perceive ladders as an obstacle. Chaucer is a Golden Retriever that lives aboard a Pearson 422. The steep ladder was very difficult for this big dog. The owners now have a home made removable ramp that makes it possible for Chaucer to get in and out on his own.

We have heard from several owners of large dogs that hip problems surface during the dogs' later years. Adding a ramp to the boat makes it possible for them to continue to cruise. Although building or carrying a ramp may not be convenient, you may want to consider trying it. Each boat is different and customizing the ramp may be the only way to get a perfect fit. Extending the time your dog can enjoy cruising with you is important to you and your pet.

The PetSTEP™ is a device that may solve some of the boarding and access problems your pet encounters. It is the only product of this type that we have found. It does have some disadvantages and it costs about $130. The PetSTEP™ is a combination ramp and utility table. We always tell people that everything on the boat has to have at least two uses. The inventor of this ramp must have been listening. It is 70 inches long when it is unfolded. This length was one of the disadvantages pointed out by some boat owners. The length is a straight run and may not accommodate an offset or angled companionway. The width is 18 inches. When used as a table, it is 28 inches high. The ramp folds in half for carrying and storing. It will support up to 500 pounds of weight. The ribbed surface reduces the likelihood of your dog slipping. The carrying weight of the ramp is 20 pounds and it has a carrying handle. Unless you are living full time on your boat and need a permanent solution to the boarding problem, the PetSTEP™ may be an excellent way to give your dog access to the boat and to below decks. We found the PetSTEP™ at the BoatUS Stores and on the Internet. Check the appendix for the websites.

Some dog owners prefer the steep ladder that makes it impossible for a small dog to climb out of the cabin. Art and Nancy own Cutter, the Schipperke we mentioned in the first chapter. One of the advantages they see in Cutter's diminutive size is that he can be carried easily under one arm, thus allowing them to determine where he will be. They believe he could climb out in an emergency, but they have discouraged the dog from thinking he can negotiate the ladder on his own.

Dinghy Access

Putting your pet on and off your boat at anchor is a challenge. A small dog or a cat is usually easy to carry aboard from a dinghy. If he is wearing a harness or PFD with a handle, lifting is quick work. When we leave the boat for a long period, we use a carrier to move our pet. Once he is established in the carrier, we can concentrate on assembling other gear, closing the boat, and other routines.

Whoever is in charge of your pet must be able to lift it from a dinghy into the boat and vice versa. It is important that this person is strong enough to negotiate lifting the pet from an unstable surface without assistance. We had friends cruising with a large German Shepherd on their powerboat. Each day she went out in the dinghy. The gate in the transom opened on to the swim platform. The dinghy was pulled alongside and made secure so the dog and other passengers could climb in easily. When they returned the process was reversed. In the afternoon, they allowed the dog to jump from the dinghy on the return trip, about fifty yards out, and swim to the platform. The dog had to stay afloat on her own until the owner came alongside. Then the dog put her front paws on the platform and the owner boosted the dog from behind. Heavy and wet, she required a strong helping hand.

A large sailboat was in our anchorage in Mexico, and the wife and springer spaniel were aboard alone. The heat was intense so she took the dog from the boat into the dinghy and then into the water. When the came time to reboard the boat, she had the wet dog in the dinghy and while attempting to lift the dog the dinghy flipped. Both of them ended up in the water with a turtled dinghy. Fortunately, several occupied boats close by heard her call for help and she and the spaniel were rescued quickly.

Daisy is a two-year old Airedale that doesn't have boarding problems. As a puppy, she was carried as you would carry a baby. Her head was facing over the shoulder and a hand over her back and rump supported her body. As she grew, she began putting her paws around John's neck when he lifted her.

Even a big dog can learn to "hang on."

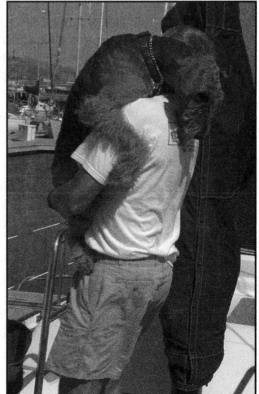

PHOTOGRAPH BY JESSIE

As an adult she puts her paws around his neck, her hind legs on his belt or waistband. John uses one hand to climb and the other to support her. John Martino said that he doesn't need to hold her but puts his hand on her back unless he needs to use it.

If you have a pet that you can't lift easily in all conditions, it is essential to make provisions for putting her on and taking her off your vessel. If you have halyards or a lifting hoist for a dinghy, making a sling for a big dog would make excellent sense. We have used our main boom and mainsheet block to lift all manner of heavy objects including our engine.

The type of dinghy you own is important when cruising with your pet. If your pet rides in the dinghy only in a carrier, almost any type of dinghy will be suitable as long as there is sufficient room for the carrier. On the other hand, if you use the dinghy every day to take your large dog(s) ashore your choices are more limited.

Stability is very important for safe boarding, riding in heavy conditions, and retrieving a pet from the water. Unless you have a large, solid dinghy such as a Boston Whaler, we think that an inflatable dinghy will be safer and less likely to sink in heavier conditions. However, the toenails of a big dog can tear or puncture some dinghy fabrics. A hard bottom inflatable or one equipped with floorboards will help protect the dinghy. If your dog boards the dinghy by scrambling over the inflated pontoons, that area will be subject to wear. You may want to reinforce this area by adding a sacrificial covering of cloth or carpet, or by using a small ramp.

Additionally, dependable power is very important if you use the dinghy every day. Some cruisers enjoy rowing, but outboards are more practical when you must contend with waves, currents, and windage. Make sure that your pet is secure before starting the engine, and avoid sudden acceleration or stops. Even with a PFD, it isn't fun to land unexpectedly in the water.

Be sure you have a dinghy painter for tying securely to a dock or your boat, and a small anchor with sufficient rode for emergencies. If you have to go into the water to rescue your pet, you need to have the dinghy stay put.

Some cruisers use small rowboats or kayaks as dinghies. This can be fun for you and your pet as long as you both wear PFD's. Not all

Sailboards aren't nearly as comfortable as the boat.

PHOTOGRAPH BY JESSIE

pets enjoy this type of experience and Foxy, our water cat, discovered this when he went for a ride on a wind surfer uninvited. The curiosity of pets combined with limited judgement can lead to surprising rides and results.

This is a story from Jim Forrest of training Cassie, an eight-year old lab, to get on and off a Catalina 36. "Even though we have a stern ladder, I felt the best place to off load her was at the rail with a drop down into the inflatable raft. The trick was to get her to go on to my lap then with her head pointed down towards the dink, I could slide her most of the way with a short drop at the end. This was encouraged by a treat dropped ahead of her that got her attention. She is a fool for a treat! She belly flopped onto the dink but came up with the treat all in one extended motion.

"This time we have to get back up on the boat from a bobbing inflatable. We had put a harness on her and I lifted and pushed while Marla pulled and lifted . . . plus, Cassie was helping too when she found out what the mission was. We all had a shower in the cockpit.

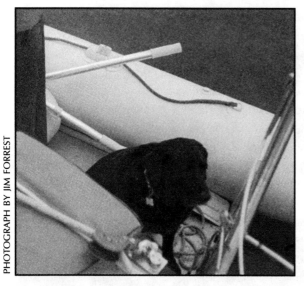

A little patience and your dog will learn how to get in and out of the dinghy.

On the next trip into doggie beach, I put Cassie in the rear of the inflatable so that I could get out before she did and thus control her and avoid the swim. By the end of the weekend she had it all figured out. She was riding around in the bow of the dingy, scampering in and out of the boat, and getting all kinds of attention from strangers."

Decks

The deck surface is important because the tread helps you to keep your footing. What do you do about your pet? The non-skid surface common on many boats has little or no affect on your pet's ability to stay on his feet. Cats with claws and dogs with nails have no means to grip this special surface. When your boat is underway that surface is not a secure walking surface for your pet. Think about how your dog or cat skids across a slick waxed surface wildly pawing to get a grip. This is the kind of grip, or lack of grip, your pet will have on a fiberglass or metal surface.

One solution we will discuss later is deck shoes/boots for your pet. The best solution for your pet and your peace of mind is to allow your pet on deck only when you are moored or the water is flat. Remember that even a passing wake can knock your pet off her feet. If you have to take your pet on deck, be sure to use a harness and leash.

Teak decks offer an advantage because they are not as slick as fiberglass or metal. Unfortunately, there is a disadvantage that you will need to overcome with a cat. The softer grain of the teak is a great place for your feline friend to scratch. Unless trained to an alternative scratching opportunity, an adult cat will do a fair amount of damage in a short time. Dogs with long toenails can severely scratch the surface. Although they won't tear a deck, the deep gouges they leave behind, particularly if they run on deck, will require maintenance.

Below deck, wood has a different finish and will have a harder surface making it less attractive for cat scratching. Wood sole boards however, will be subject to scratching from long canine nails. Furthermore, they can be very slippery if highly varnished. Rugs or carpeted surfaces are kinder to your pet and are more easily replaced if they are damaged. Cleaning rugs and carpets should be a regular—daily—event to keep them free of hair and smelling fresh. We use a damp sponge on the upholstery, sweeping it onto the carpet. Then we vacuum up the offending hair. A quick spray of commercial freshener or diluted white vinegar cleans up the smelly locations and improves the boat's environment. You can buy household deodorants produced specifically for pets at your local pet supply store or supermarket.

Deck Protection

"O.B." or Obi is a Lhasa Apso on our dock. He acquired his name on his first boat day. Cherie explained that the first time the dog was on deck, he raced from the bow to the stern and kept going, overboard. They think the excited dog thought the water was the parking lot. It is hard to know what pets are thinking. In this case, you might wonder if he was thinking at all.

Just as some boats have netting in the lifelines to protect a child or sail from going overboard, netting may help keep your pet aboard in rough weather. You can buy a commercial netting to string in the lifelines or it is easy albeit time consuming to thread line through your lifelines. The peace of mind is the reward for your effort.

Many cruising sailboats have lee clothes to protect the cockpit. These may also help protect your pet when things get rough. However, the cloths should not get in the way of trimming your sails easily and should not make lines and blocks difficult to adjust.

Powerboat bulwarks are solid enough to keep most pets protected from washing overboard. Open bows on smaller boats are difficult to enclose. It is more practical not to allow your pet to go forward. Just as with a human, if it is necessary to be on deck when conditions are not safe, then your pet needs to be fitted with a personal flotation device (PFD).

Access to Shelter

Earlier we mentioned getting access via a ramp to the cabin or a gangway to the deck. Once on board, your pet needs to be able to move about to find protection from the sun, to have access to her food and water, and a comfortable lounging space on deck.

If your boat is all on one level, then your pet will be able to come and go without assistance. Unfortunately, most boats are multilevel and access may be limited. With kittens and puppies it is easiest and most desirable to pick up your baby and move him to the location you want him to use. This establishes specific locations for specific uses, teaches your pet that handling is part of his routine, and allows you to exercise some control. However, if your puppy is going to grow beyond the easy to carry size, you may not want him to become used to that mode of transportation.

If there are specific areas that you don't want your pet to have access to, he must learn that immediately. The engine room is not a safe place for any pet at any time. Riding on a side deck or on the bow is generally not a good practice. For cats, the inclination to climb on sail covers, dodgers, or any other canvas product should be discouraged, just as you would discourage your cat from climbing drapes at home. Mancha learned as a young cat to jump from the main boom onto the dodger. It was a cute trick until the day the dodger cloth gave way and he fell through. He was embarrassed and his owners were faced with acquiring a new dodger—not a small expense—or a smaller cat.

Give your pet a designated outside spot to enjoy warm days and to be with you. Small dogs and cats seem to fit anywhere. Putting your 100-pound dog into a niche is not as easy. Many cruisers accommodate their cat or dog with a basket or bed in a protected deck space as well as below. Using a nonskid rug or placing a nonskid mat under a basket will create a more secure spot.

Many sailboat cruisers with large dogs do not permit their dog to come below deck. On a small boat where it is difficult to accommodate a large dog, the dog eats, sleeps, and cruises on deck. Typically a dodger and bimini combine to provide protection from rain and sun. Others would rather have the dog below and close to them regardless of cramped quarters. Choosing whether your dog will be a cabin or deck dog is a matter of space and comfort. Don't ignore your pet's need for space and shelter.

Space for Your Pet

A friend gave us a basket for our cat. It was woven wicker in the shape of a beehive. It had an entry hole that was at a perfect height for the cat to curl up and peek out, undetected. Unfortunately, the basket was small and the cat soon opted to sleep elsewhere and have more legroom. He had a passion for empty boxes, which we don't normally have on the boat, and insisted on having one in which to hide.

Pets like routines and feel more comfortable with predictable behavior from you. That doesn't mean that everyone should be doing the same thing with his or her pet. We don't sleep the same hours, eat the same foods, or enjoy the same music. Your pet is the same.

Having said that, it is clear that pets expect certain behavior from us. If we regularly feed them in the morning and then forget, they aren't likely to let us ignore them. If their favorite blanket or pillow suddenly disappears into the laundry or the trash, they search for the missing object until we provide a substitute they can accept.

Cats like their own place, but it may not be where you expected.

PHOTOGRAPH BY JESSIE

Cruising means having those things that your animal has come to expect. If you always put food in a certain location at a specific time, you need to follow the pattern. If you can't maintain a time schedule, try to maintain the location. Alternatively, if you have to change the location try to maintain the timing.

Many cruisers find that the crate or kennel they use for transporting the dog to and from the boat works well as the dog's berth on the boat. Fastening or wedging the carrier into an out-of-the-way spot will give the dog a "home." Just as you sometimes want a child to "go to your room," a dog may be noisy, excited, misbehaving, or tired and need to retire to his room. The crate can be your dog's refuge from the world, a secure place to nap, and a place to send your cranky pet. A crate can provide a place to be sent so the dog understands how to get out from underfoot.

In planning for your pet, remember also, that you will need space for his personal belongings. For a dog or cat, you will need a place to store sufficient food. If you are using dry food, be sure you store it in a dry place. Large quantities can be stored in a garbage can with a fitted lid. Smaller quantities will fit in large plastic storage bins or jars. Pet food in cans will rust if it is aboard for a long period. Dip the tops and bottoms of the cans in paraffin or paint them with varnish to protect them from rusting. As with all your other provisions, secure your pet food so that it remains stowed where you put it. You don't want the motion of the waves or a wake to rearrange your stores.

Puppies & Kittens

For long term cruising, I think it is important to start with a puppy or kitten. If your pet learns from the beginning to live on a boat, then you will have fewer obstacles to overcome. Most of the foregoing applies to adults and juveniles as well as infants. With puppies and kittens, you need to make a special plan.

There are some destructive behaviors in which kittens and puppies love to indulge. Train them not to perform these behaviors except on prescribed items. Puppies love to chew on anything available. Just as you would at home, you need to train your puppy to chew on the chewing toys and not on shoes, fenders, joinery, or lifejackets. You will need to keep these toys available on the boat, and carefully monitor your puppy.

Kittens love to scratch to keep their claws husked and sharpened. We have seen major damage done by the sweetest of fluff balls. Many cats ignore the standard scratching post or it doesn't appeal to them. On a boat, a piece of line is an attractive item for scratching but not all lines are the same. We found a piece of sisal line satisfied our cat. Boca had begun to scratch on the newly acquired mainsheet. A piece of sisal wound tightly around the steering pedestal was immediately better from the cat's point of view. It was always in the same place, no one bothered him when he used it, it was high enough to permit a good stretch, and the praise was formidable.

Cats use their hind claws for fighting and need to kick and scratch with those hind claws. In wrestling with a littermate or in fighting, the cat will grab his opponent with his front feet and kick with the back feet. He needs to mimic that type of action as part of his exercise and game playing. An old, heavy carpet or towel that is available satisfies a cat's need to kick. As with the sisal, the carpet always needs to be in the same place, and using it needs to be allowed.

Kittens and puppies need to be "boat trained" immediately to keep peace in the family. Kittens will adapt to a litter box immediately.

PHOTOGRAPH BY JESSIE

A permanent scratching post for your cat will save upholstery and clothes.

Make sure that the box is where the kitten can find it and use it. It can be small to begin with and should be some distance from where the kitten eats. It also needs to be where it won't tip over and things are not likely to fall in it in rough seas.

Puppies need paper initially on a boat until they develop some control and are leash trained. In a later chapter, we will discuss training dogs to eliminate on command. This training can begin in puppyhood as soon as she understands the use of the leash.

Babies sleep best when cuddled or sleeping in an enclosed area. The same is true with kittens and puppies. Provide a small comfortable place to sleep within earshot or arm's length. This is reassuring to a brand new pet. Within a night or two, the pet will feel secure. Be sure that you don't encourage her to stay awake or play. There is nothing worse than being awakened nightly by a frolicsome pet that wants a playmate.

Play with your pet regularly—during the waking hours—to encourage her physical development and to teach her what to expect from you. Games of fetch are fun but confined spaces are not a good place to teach them unless your puppy is small. Puppies are great with a Kong-style toy (a chew toy that dispenses treats). Kittens love feathery light toys to pounce on or small toys to attack. Be sure that playing involves objects rather than your hands and feet. Cats have difficulty knowing that biting or attacking as a kitten is not good adult behavior, and as adults, the potential damage from their teeth and claws is severe.

Puppies and kittens usually need to eat smaller amounts and sometimes require more frequent feedings. Napping normally follows eating with young pets. Plan your feeding times accordingly and work into a practical schedule for you and your new pet. Remember that as your kitten matures he will become truer to his species and develop a nocturnal pattern. We found with our cats that they eat the most food at night and they prowl every nook and cranny at night; this nocturnal activity is called standing watch. During daylight hours, your adult cat will spend most of her time sleeping.

Remember that your puppy or kitten's small size prevents getting off the boat or out of the cabin temporarily. When you discover that your baby is about to leap up the ladder or tries to jump into the water, have his brand new harness at the ready.

Animal Care and Upkeep

4 Many cruisers regard their boat time as unfettered. There is no schedule, no plan, and no order. Certainly a little chaos in our lives is a relief from the work routine. Unfortunately, many of us have learned that absolute disorder leads to absolute chaos. Your pet does not appreciate chaos when it leads to discomfort. Certain activities cannot be put off or ignored.

Grooming

Not shaving or taking a bath is a type of rebellion we frequently practice on cruising holidays. Our dermatologist endorses "less bathing" because the skin does not dry out when natural oils aren't washed away. He does insist, however, on sun protection. Our fascination with bathing is less a natural phenomenon and more a social expectation. We found that if no one bathes, no one notices, and vice versa. We do think cleanliness is important for health, so we wash hands and faces, comb hair, and brush teeth regularly. A bath every few days is pleasant. Your pet can manage with a similar routine. Your cat needs brushing and expects it. Your dog doesn't like ticks or a salt encrusted face. You do have an obligation to give your pets the care and attention that they need, but relax.

Summer holidays are usually warm and sunny. You and your kids wear shorts, get short haircuts, and relax. Unfortunately, your pets can't do the same, but you can provide them summer relief. Many dogs have haircuts as a regular event. This clipping that is regarded as proper for the breed, is another social phenomenon. Just as human hair fashion is a social expectation, dog clips are an expectation. Some of the extremes in clips are for shows. Other clipping styles are functional, just as their names proclaim: puppy cut, kennel cut, etc. Some clipping styles are exaggerations of cuts that were once practical for the activities the dog was bred for . . . poodles for example. Dog breeds that don't shed a heavy coat, are usually the groups that are clipped.

Dogs that shed typically have acquired an undercoat to insulate them in cold weather. As the weather becomes warmer, they naturally lose that hair. One veterinarian told me about two Huskies that were show dogs. Each winter they went to Minnesota to develop the deepest possible coat. In the spring, the dogs made the rounds of shows in warmer latitudes before losing the luxurious coat. The density of the coat is a direct result of their environment. If you go cruising in a year-round warm climate, you will discover that your pet will develop little or no insulating coat.

You can indeed give your pooch a summer cut if heat is a problem. Dogs pant to perspire. If you reduce the thickness of the coat, it will help cool your dog. For your holiday of a month or less in a hot climate, a single clip before your departure should be sufficient to keep your dog cool. If you think your dog will suffer in the hot weather, your veterinarian can make recommendations on improving the situation. Clipping a dog without knowing what is best can lead to a sunburned dog.

Sunburn can be a problem with albinotic pets. These are pets with white skin, pink eyes, pink noses, and pink paw pads. Wherever there

is a lack of pigment in the skin, sunburn is possible. Dogs with very little hair and white skin need sun protection. Sun blocking creams can be used, but the best protection is to stay out of the sun. Since animals (particularly cats) lick

If hot weather is a problem, give your pooch a haircut.

their fur, ask your veterinarian's advice on non-toxic sun block cream if you are going to use one.

One final note on clipping, cats don't pant and they do shed. However, a cat with an extremely dense coat that is suddenly cruising in a hot climate could have problems. If your cat is not adjusting to the heat, then cutting its hair can help. Before resorting to a hair cut, give your cat a thorough brushing to see if that improves the cooling process. Aesthetically, a clipped cat may look strange, but he will be alive. If your cat begins to pant, he's too hot and needs relief. Use ice packs and try getting him to take water. Some cats will lick ice cubes. However, you may even have to resort to a dropper to get liquid into your cat. We have bathed cats in cool water, but it is not normally a feline's preference.

Brushing your dog or cat daily is the greatest service and kindness you can do. A comb, a brush, and a towel are your basic tools for grooming. If you don't choose to clip your pooch, plan to brush at least once a day. As we indicated, shedding is a normal condition with warm weather. Combing and brushing daily

A Persian needs daily brushing to reduce shedding and hair balls.

PHOTOGRAPH BY KAY MALSEED

will speed up the process and keep your boat cleaner. Do your grooming on deck with your pet facing upwind. The loose hair will blow away from the face making the job of brushing easier. After a good comb and brushing, wipe your pet's coat with a towel to pickup the rest of the loose hair. It will also remove the loose dander on your dog's coat and the dried saliva from the cat's fur. Most pets will come to enjoy this daily ritual since it focuses your undivided attention on them.

Particularly for longhaired cats, daily brushing will decrease the amount of fur the cat ingests when she cleans herself. This should decrease the incidence of hairballs, which are unpleasant to clean up after whether you are on a boat or land. Schooner is living aboard S/V Wave Rider in the South Pacific. Her owner reports, "Schooner will be 11 years old in October this year, is a flame-colored Persian who weighs 11 lbs. (10 lbs. hair/1 lb. meat we tell the natives). He is responsible for our Island Packet 35 being lined with fur. He needs to be brushed daily to avoid hairballs; we use Sargeant's cat hairball remedy, if necessary." Living with longhaired cats requires a supply of hairball medicine be on hand regardless of where you cruise.

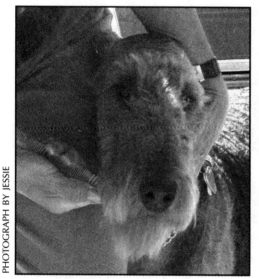

PHOTOGRAPH BY JESSIE

Use a comb to keep curly hair groomed.

Dogs that swim daily as part of their exercise routine need brushing before they get wet. This loosens hair and dander to slough off. Then rinse and brush them after swimming. Whether you are swimming in salt or fresh water, rinse yourself and your pet with water from a hose or shower afterwards. Swimming in saltwater leaves salt on the fur and can create skin problems. In addition, licking salty fur is hard on the digestive system.

Some cats will play in the water but don't assume that your cat is one of them. We had a cat who thought he was a Labrador Retriever and swam after ducks. He began to groom immediately upon climbing back on the boat. We stepped in and rinsed the cat with fresh water because we didn't want him to lick the salt from his fur. He did not swim on a regular basis but he didn't resist going in the water.

On some boats, water is a restricted commodity. We find a garden sprayer with a small shower attachment works fine for humans and pets. Typically, the sprayer holds about three gallons and is portable so that you can use it anywhere on the boat. If you have a freshwater hose-down unit on your boat, regulate the pressure before you rinse your pet right off the boat. Don't point pressurized water from a hose directly at your pet's face.

Long term cruising and long passages require more planning. Your pets will need daily grooming. Bathing is not practical underway and should be avoided. Dry shampoo products may do more harm than good. Remember that residue from a dry shampoo could cause skin problems. Brushing is important regardless of whether or not you bathe your dog. The comb, brush, and towel will remove loose hair and dirt. Doing it regularly keeps you aware of your pet's skin condition as well as showing attention and affection.

When your cat finishes grooming, rub the fur lightly with a towel to remove the dried saliva deposited by his tongue. It leaves the coat shining, and you have less cleaning to do. Be sure there is always plenty of water available for your cat to replenish his system.

Manicures

Cats on board need their claws. Their ability to climb and react to the boat's motion depends upon holding on. If you are starting with a house cat that has been declawed, be sure to provide her with a safe haven below and on deck. Without claws, your cat will be helpless in many situations and should wear a harness below decks and a PFD on deck, in the dinghy, and boarding.

If you have a choice, leave your cat's claws intact. You can learn to take care of the claws and minimize any damage that they might do. We mentioned in chapter three creating a permanent scratching location. Your cat needs to scratch to remove the old husking from her claws. We use a sisal wrapped surface easily accessed by our cat; it has saved clothing, upholstery, brightwork, and sheets. Remember that a cat will return to a specific location if you are consistent. Each time your kitten or cat begins to scratch in the wrong location, pick her up and move her to the scratching place. Put her claws on the rope to indicate what you want. Most cats get the picture quickly, especially with praise. As long as the scratching post is maintained, the cat will be satisfied.

In addition to the scratching your cat normally does, it is a good idea to clip your cat's claws on a regular basis. By taking the sharp

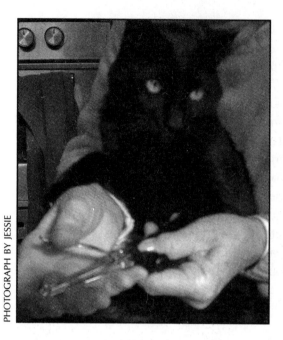

Cats need a regular manicure in addition to a scratching post.

points only, your cat can still climb and cling, but she will do less damage. She won't pull threads on fabric surfaces or accidentally scratch you. Use a pair of cat clippers or a small nail clipper. It is essential to work quickly and carefully to avoid a struggle with your cat. I hold the cat on my lap just as I would a baby. This has been an acceptable position since he was a small kitten. This allows me to control the cat with my arms and work quickly with my hands. Gently squeeze the paw until the claws extend, and then quickly clip just the outer curl of the tip. We don't clip the back claws because they don't do as much damage. You can forego clipping the back claws if your cat doesn't want to cooperate.

Dogs need manicures when they are on board for any length of time. Running about on hard surfaces or exercising with you at home may keep your dog's nails worn down. Dogs with nails that turn down wear on hard surfaces. Many dogs have nails that turn up and no amount of running will wear this type of nail down. Since there are no hard surfaces to run on aboard a boat, your dog's nails are likely to become unmanageable quickly.

If you are planning to take your dog cruising, start manicures before you go so the dog has a chance to adjust. Long nails are a hazard because they will catch on lines and gear. Tearing the nail is painful and will require first aid. If you haven't tried clipping her nails, have your groomer or veterinarian show you the best method.

Dog nail clippers are the easiest way to get the job done. If your dog is used to being held or will stay on command, clipping is easy.

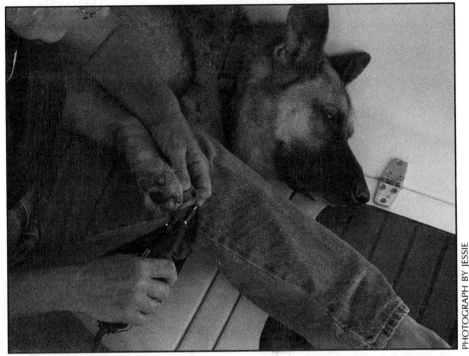

PHOTOGRAPH BY JESSIE

Tyler's heavy nails are manicured with a Dremel tool.

Sometimes manicuring a big dog is better done with two people. One person holding the dog while the other does the clipping. Large dogs such as Tyler, a 110 pound German Shepherd, have thick, heavy nails. Clippers are not always up to the task if you can't apply sufficient leverage. Christine Dowler uses a Dremel tool™ for manicures on Tyler.

Let your dog become familiar with the tool and the noise. Select a small grinder that best accommodates your dog's nails. If you are comfortable doing the job, your dog will be comfortable, too. Be careful using the electric tool.

It is better to clip just a short length of nail than to cut too deeply and cut into the quick. Be patient and gentle with your pet, cat or dog, when clipping her nails. If she is nervous, do just one paw at a time. If you do cut into the quick, a dab from a styptic pencil will control the bleeding.

Pets do sense from you when something is a "big deal" so it is important for you to have a positive and relaxed attitude. Speak softly to your pet. Yelling at her to "hold still" is likely to make matters much worse. Praise and affection following a new routine are important, and sometimes a treat for the pet makes the effort worthwhile.

Dental Care

Dental treatment for pets is still a new idea for many pet owners. It is important because cats and dogs develop problems without fanfare and we can't teach them to brush twice a day. Fortunately, we don't fill our pets with sugar. Cavities are not nearly the issue that they are for humans. Diseases that attack the gums are a serious threat to pets. They can result in loss of teeth, infection, and the spread of infection to other parts of the body. Checking teeth and watching for the development of plaque—the teeth become yellow and brown—is very important.

Plaque is a familiar term to most of us. Advertisements for various toothpaste and toothbrushes have made the public knowledgeable about dental hygiene. Plaque on your pet's teeth may not be familiar, but it can be a problem. It can lead to gum disease. Plaque develops over a period, so those who go offshore or don't have ready access to veterinary services are those most likely to let plaque go undiscovered and untreated.

At home, there are plaque fighting treats, the veterinarian can scrape the plaque, and you can buy your dog or cat a toothbrush. The latter may sound like overkill, but it is a simple solution to keeping your pet's mouth healthy.

Brushing teeth isn't easy, but it is important to you pet's health.

If you can't buy special treats or see the veterinarian regularly, your only option for dental care is to do regular dental cleaning.

We have two different types of brushes that we have used. One is a thimble-like plastic cap that fits on your fingertip. Use it on the row of incisors, the small teeth at the front of the mouth, on the upper and lower jaw of your dog or cat. The thimble is easy to use because it fits on your finger and it allows you better control of your pet's mouth.

The second brush has a handle and brush head. Use this brush on the large molars, top and bottom, at the back of the jaw. The molars are harder to reach because they requires holding the lips apart to insert the brush. Cats are not particularly cooperative in this venture; some dogs have been trained to smile through the ordeal. Initially, dental care was a two-person task for us, but once the cat accepted the inevitability of brushing, one person could manage. Dogs reportedly are more patient and willing than their feline friends.

Be sure to ask your veterinarian about dental procedures. If you expect to be absent for more than six months, ask if scraping is necessary, and have it done before your departure. Schooner has had professional teeth cleaning by the veterinarian several times; anesthetic is used. This scraping process is expensive because it does involve anesthesia. If the veterinarian recommends brushing, be sure to buy and learn how to use the necessary tools before you leave.

We Don't Live on Fish

5 Cruisers do not live off the sea. There are still a few dreamers who think in those terms, but reality dictates that we plan and provision for our weekend trip or ocean voyage. This means that you need to make plans for your pet's provisions as well as your own. We recognize there is a big difference in planning for the extremes mentioned, but even an overnight cruise requires some planning.

What do you feed your pet?

The first rule in feeding your pet or your crew is the same. Feed them what they are used to eating. There is nothing so certain as the health problems that arise from introducing a new diet. When we say diet it is all-inclusive—food, water, and treats.

If your cat or dog likes a specific flavor or brand of food, then that is what you should take. If your pet prefers dry food to wet food, then respect his preference. If he is accustomed to treats of a certain type or at a specific time, then follow the routine. Maintain your feeding routine as faithfully as possible. Constipation is common among humans and pets when voyages start. Drinking as much liquid as possible is generally the best preventative for humans. A preventative method for your pet is to add fiber to his diet. Pumpkin is a great source of fiber. Add a small quantity of canned pumpkin to your dog or cat's food. If your pet's diet is normally of the dry variety, buy or make a small amount of wet food and mix the pumpkin into it. You may have to use special attention to encourage a finicky eater to try this new taste.

Be sure that you have enough food for the planned cruise and then add a few extra days supply. Delays caused by bad weather or mechanical problems are a normal part of cruising. Assuming problems can't happen to you, is a good way to invite disaster. We discussed earlier the need for sufficient space on your boat, emergency rations, and supplies will occupy some of that space.

Some pets are on special diets that have been recommended by the veterinarian. Eating prescribed diets isn't just an issue of pleasing your pet but a matter of keeping her healthy as well. Although pets are increasingly common on boats, don't assume that the store that carries bread, milk, and beer will have what you need. You may find yourself in a tiny general store on Lake Huron or in a small native store on St. Lucia, where no one has ever heard of Science Diet™ or Iams™. Take that extra box or bag along, just in case.

Most of us believe that cats are the most finicky eaters on the planet. Actually, they come in just behind our seven-year old granddaughter. Unless you want to live with an angry feline, put the Whiskas™ or Cat Chow™ in the provisions along with the peanut butter. Don't alter the routine your cat enjoys and expects.

Along with the food, depending on your pet's eating habits, taking a supply of favorite treats and the water she normally drinks is a good idea. Water is a problem for humans and pets. With your pet, remember how important drinking water is to her overall health. If the water is unfamiliar and your cat or dog refuses to drink it or the water makes her sick, you have a problem. Earlier when we discussed adjustment to the boat, drinking the water on the boat is part of that process. If you think you will have to refill your water tank in an unknown location, set aside water from the tap on the boat or the one at home. Depending upon the size of your animal, you may need a couple of jerry

PHOTOGRAPH BY KING ARTHUR FLOUR COMPANY

Treats are important to cruisers including the four-footed ones.

cans. On a short cruising holiday, precautions as simple as reserve water improve the quality of your holiday and your pet's holiday.

Treats for your pet don't need to be commercial food. In fact, veterinarians recommend healthy treats that you might ordinarily carry for yourself. Dogs love raw carrots, grapes, and a whole range of fruits and vegetables. Our cat is always exploring and finds raw mushrooms and raw spinach irresistible. Giving your pet a diet of commercial treats is probably unnecessary.

Long Term or Long Distance Food Problems

Long term cruising presents a different set of problems. Once you leave your local area, your native land, or your hemisphere, many things will be different. Until recently, there were many countries where no pet food was available. Pets were food. In some places, they still are. I am squeamish and just seeing cats and dogs held in cages for sale in the market is very unpleasant.

We asked several of the long distance cruisers how they managed pet food. According to Tania Aebi, "When the going was good, we would be visiting a country with a market for cat food. When times were lean, he ate rice, tomato paste and tuna stews with me. We also ate other things straight from cans that he liked: asparagus, sardines, wieners, soups. For a cat, he had a very open mind about food without abandoning his essential catiness. He maintained a constant deck watch for stranded flying fish and squid that supplemented his dietary needs very nicely. One time, in the middle of the North Atlantic, he even caught and heartlessly devoured an exhausted and unsuspecting canary."

Kay Malseed is careful about Schooner's health. "Schooner enjoys his prescription Hills Science Diet™ (CDs) for neutered males—which has eliminated UTI's of his past—yet we carry Amoxicillin as a precaution. We purchased ample quantities during visits to the US and, fortunately, found it available in Panama and Tahiti. His diet is augmented with fresh caught/boiled fish and occasional Friskies™ moist canned food and dried food. He has been in remarkable good health—probably because he does not associate with other animals."

Pearl on S/V *Oddly Enough* is not big on fish. "Kibbles are the basis of her diet; she used to get a small can of cat food every other evening, but since getting out of range of Fancy Feast, she hasn't found anything she likes enough to eat consistently, including sardines. She gets fish scraps when we have them (Mahi Mahi being her favorite), and otherwise is not a big eater, she is a small cat," according to owner Ann Hoffner.

Mary Iverson reports that her cats discovered a new batch of alfalfa sprouts and thought they were terrific. Many cats living on land will chew on grass and other vegetation. Local pet stores sell seeded tubs so you can grow small quantities of grass for your housecat to munch. The ancient cats on the desert found moisture in vegetation so it isn't an unusual behavior for your cat to enjoy eating growing plants. In fact, your cat may prefer the moisture in a plant to a plain bowl of water.

Foreign travel means stockpiling huge quantities of food, especially for a dog, or adjusting your pet's diet. The first time I went on line in search of a recipe for kitten food, the first response was "Where in the world are you going that you can't buy pet food?" After explaining that I couldn't plan on availability once out of the US, I was offered a simple recipe based on food that we would typically have on hand. With the addition of a vitamin supplement that I bought before we left, the food met the dietary requirements. The difficulty was to make it something the kitten enjoyed; that was the challenge. The kitten grew up as a gourmet omnivore.

Boat Made Pet Food

Before you set off with ingredients in hand to prepare pet food, you need to practice making the food and testing the food with your pet. Since boat-made food is freshly prepared, and therefore made frequently, you don't want to get your pet accustomed to food that is difficult to prepare. You will need to prepare food every few days. It is possible to can food but it is complicated and you introduce jars that may break. Also, there are more health risks when canning meat-based foods than when putting up pickles or jam. You don't want your pet to get food poisoning when you are days away from a veterinarian. If you are equipped with a freezer, meal sized plastic pouches might work. We've not had that luxury in our cruising. Again, don't assume these recipes or methods will work. Make them and try them out with your pet before you begin your voyage.

"People food" is frequently full of fats and sugars that we shouldn't eat. Likewise filling pets with sugars and fats is not healthy. Cats and dogs do not have the same dietary requirements as humans or each other, therefore avoid feeding your pets scraps from the table. While convenient, it can ultimately lead to serious health problems for your pet.

Dogs are omnivores and do very well on a variety of foods. One popular diet recently touted for dogs was the lamb and rice diet. The only ones who are likely to benefit from this diet are the people who manufacture it. It is very inexpensive to make and is full of fat. It does make clear one point. A mixture of rice, pasta, and protein with vitamin supplements is easy to make. If you anticipate a long passage, or a long period away from provisioning stops, stocking up on rice, pasta, some canned meats, poultry, and fish will give you the basics for your dog. The rice and pasta need to be cooked, but the protein can be used directly from the can. If you have refrigeration, prepare enough food for several days. If you don't have refrigeration or are conserving power, daily preparation using your propane stove is more practical.

High sodium content is common in canned goods, so be sure you keep fresh water available for your dog to dilute the salt. Although we use salt water as a fresh water, cooking substitute on long passages, we do use a quick fresh water rinse on food boiled in salt water. We do this to reduce the quantity of sodium we consume.

Cats are carnivores. They require a larger percentage of protein in their diet than their canine cousins do. If you catch fish for food, your cat will insist that you share it. It is tempting to give tidbits of fresh fish to your cat while cleaning and preparation is under way. Please explain to your cat—we find it helps—that cooked meat, fish, and poultry, is what the veterinarian recommends.

Many people fear giving cats organ meats such as heart, kidney, liver, and spleen. These are all acceptable foods when cooked thoroughly. Never consume intestines or give them to your pets. The intestines harbor the parasites that live in mammals, birds, and fish.

Even cooked, it is possible for the parasite or its eggs to survive, and be ingested by your pet.

One favorite food of cats is a mixture of cooked ground meat and cooked liver with rice. Again, include vitamin supplements in the diet to make it balanced. *From North to the Night*, this is Alvah Simon's recipe for the cat food. He fed it to Halifax, his cat, while iced in at Tay Bay above the Arctic Circle.

"One day, as she walked from the bag bottom over the length of my body to get out for some fresh air, I noticed that she felt surprisingly light. I had not stocked much cat food, thinking that she could eat what we ate, but no matter her hunger, she would not touch the smoked meats. I turned on an electric light and saw that she was alarmingly thin. In the energy-demanding Arctic, one can starve to death almost as quickly as one can die of thirst.

"I searched for the best medium with which to convey fat into her little stomach. For the baking of bread, the *Joy of Cooking* told me to "let dough rise at room temperature for two hours." I took one look at the thermometer and devised Plan B. I took the full mixing bowl into the sleeping bag, hoping to use my cocoon and body heat as a proofing oven. It was a slow process. I fell asleep, rolled over, and spread the gooey mess everywhere. I woke to find Halifax licking the slop off my face. For my next attempt, I wrapped the dough bowl and a hot-water bottle in a woolen blanket. Maybe I checked its progress too often, because the result was a loaf with the texture of oak through which even feline fangs could not cut. The effect of the gas blowtorch on the next globule was equally discouraging.

"Finally, I put the dough in a body-warmed bread pan, put it in the insulated oven, placed a lit candle beside it, and closed the oven. This worked too well. The goo grew like an alien life form and filled the oven to its blackened confines. I scraped out the sooty mess with a spatula. Experimenting, I adjusted the amount of yeast to an exact length of candle stub. Just as the candle went out, I turned the oven on. In this way, I economically produced some handsome loaves of white, wheat, oat corn-meal, onion flake, and combinations thereof. Halifax did not offer up a purr easily through those dark days, but a bowl of warm diced bread saturated with butter and oily tuna evoked at least a hint of grateful rumble."

He does admit to splurging once, allowing Halifax to eat an entire can of tuna on Christmas Day. As we discovered in the letter from Mary, he indeed would go to whatever lengths were required to satisfy Halifax.

If you expect to make food for your pet, get vitamin and mineral supplement information from your veterinarian. Be sure that you have a generic name for the supplements so that you can locate more in foreign countries. It is essential that your pet take vitamin supplements if you are making food for it. Typically, dogs will eat food laced with whatever medication or vitamin you want them to have. If your dog isn't fussy, putting the medicine on top of the food makes it disappear quickly. If the medicine has a strong odor, or your dog is a fussy eater, mix the medicine in a small amount of food. Feed that food first when the dog is truly hungry and follow up with the untreated remainder.

Cats are more determined about avoiding medicines. Some pills can be pulverized and mixed into your cat's food. More often, the cat will walk away from the mixture. Give your cat liquids with a dropper or place the pill in its mouth and hold the mouth closed. If the cat doesn't swallow, blow gently on its nose and it will reflexively swallow. We find that preceding the meal immediately with the medicine conditions the cat. The cat learns that food follows medicine. Where medicine is concerned, always check with your veterinarian for the best methods of administration.

Recipes

There are some recipes you might want to try on your pet while you still have access to commercially produced pet foods. If you are going to need an emergency or fallback resource, doing some advance testing will be worth your while.

I've listed in the website appendix a resource for a dog biscuit mix. It is a product of the King Arthur Flour Company. It contains whole grains, dried whole eggs, brewers yeast, beef extract, cracked flaxseed, garlic, and parsley. The latter two items are in small amounts. This mix requires your addition of water, a small amount of vegetable oil, and some powdered yeast. This particular product does not use sugar and has only a tiny amount of salt. It will work well for a treat or, if necessary, a training reinforcement. Although this is a dog biscuit mix, we found that our cat and some of his dock mates liked it as well. Remember when you make these biscuits, they must be of a size appropriate to your pet's mouth. Cats will insist on biscuits being broken into pieces. We found that pulverizing the biscuits into a granola like consistency increased feline appeal.

One veterinarian suggested this recipe for cats. You should experiment with this one as some cats aren't fond of beef liver and may want calf, lamb, or poultry liver:

Cook one pound of ground beef and a quarter pound of liver until there is no pink color. Chop or process the cooked meat. Add a cup of cooked rice that has no salt, a teaspoon of vegetable oil, and a teaspoon of calcium carbonate. Mix well. When you are ready to serve your cat, add a few drops of a feline vitamin supplement, which your veterinarian can help you find. Some vitamins have a strong odor that seems to get stronger if it is combined with the whole quantity of cat food when you make it.

PHOTOGRAPH BY KING ARHTUR FLOUR COMPANY

Making dog biscuits is easy with this mix.

A recipe that our neighbor uses with Murray, his small mixed breed dog was developed because the dog was aging and having some difficulty digesting food. Although we thought the dog was being finicky, he seemed to thrive and his housemate retriever, thought the food was good.

Cook a whole chicken in water without salt. Bone the chicken completely and throw away innards, and skin. The organ meat should be cooked thoroughly if you plan to include it. Use remaining broth to cook two cups of rice. One cup of dry rice cooked with two cups of liquid will yield approximately two cups of cooked rice. Add a package of frozen peas with the rice while it cooks. Cool and combine the rice and pea mixture with the meat. If you are feeding a small dog, make sure that the pieces of meat are manageable. This is a soft diet so it is important that your dog have some hard chews as well. The dog biscuit mix we mentioned will make a good supplement. In fact, our neighbor's dog is now my best friend since he discovered I was the source of dog biscuits.

Most veterinarians have resources for homemade pet foods. You do need to practice making the foods and finding out which ones work. Some form of poultry, eggs, rice, and meats are universally available. Using goat or lamb may not be familiar, but it is satisfactory eating. In some places, bulgar wheat may be more available than rice. The aroma of the food is important to your pet. We found fresh dried peas in Australia and New Zealand that tasted like fresh peas when they were re-hydrated.

Robin Graham fed his blind kitten, Fili, milk everyday. Although he said that it didn't agree with her—she threw up every night—she liked drinking it. Many cats are lactose intolerant and can become very sick when given milk. Avoid it unless your certain it agrees with your cat. If you have a cat that likes milk and manages it, you can purchase ultra heat-treated (UHT) milk. It comes in a box, is easy to store, and does not require refrigeration until it is opened. Our cat, at age seven, insists on milk each morning; he drinks about two ounces of the UHT non-fat milk. Since we use milk all the time, cruising or in port, we find this packaging very convenient. If you can't find it in your grocery store, we have listed the Net Grocer website as a source. Most foreign countries have this milk available in stores, but it is harder to find in the USA.

Dishes and Utensils

Your pet thrives on consistency. If the dishes you use at home will work on the boat, then take them along. Even if this is a weekend jaunt and you plan to use paper plates, think about how to make it familiar for your pet. If water to do dishes is an issue, try using a paper bowl or plate at home for a few days, before you start on your cruise. Your pet will have the opportunity to adjust to the new bowl, and you will discover if your pet eats paper plates and bowls. Chaucer, the boot wearing Golden Retriever, eats anything that he can chew into digestible bits. If you make the change in a familiar location then it will be less unsettling. Remember that you want your pet to maintain normal eating habits in order to maintain normal elimination and maintain good health.

For longer trips or holidays, use plastic or metal dishes for your pet. The self-watering or feeding dishes are fine if you can weight them or fasten them in place. A dish of water or food has a lower center of gravity than the feeders. Again, if you must change the routine, do it at home first. Some pets have a problem with plastic containers, so be sure to check it out at home.

The plastic or vinyl nonskid place mats that you use on your dinette table keep your plates from sliding with boat motion. Those mats are just as effective under your pet's bowls to help keep them in place. Of course, a heeling sailboat is difficult. If we know that the angle will be only for a short time, we can empty the dishes. Pets need to have access to water, and going twelve hours is really stretching the limits. Food is not as important, but even a handheld snack will help your pet get through a rough afternoon on the water.

One of the changes you can make so that food and water are contained is to use deeper bowls. You need to be realistic about your pet's reach or he is likely to put a foot into the bowl to get closer to the food. A better solution may be to put a smaller quantity of food and water into the regular, pet-food dishes. If your pet is hungry enough to empty them, it is easier to refill the bowls than mop up a mess.

Our local BoatUS store has a water dish that is practically spill proof. The Buddy Bowl™ has a cone or funnel sitting in a large dish that resembles the ordinary pet dish. The bottom of this insert is open. The water is poured into the surrounding dish, and it rises to a uniform level in the dish and the cone. If the dish tilts the water flows to the low side of the dish. This action empties the cone so that it does not spill out. It may not be practical in extreme condition. You will find the website for the Buddy Bowl™ in the appendix. They come in two sizes. The small one is about $10 and the big one is $14. The advertising maintains that the bowl can turn over completely without spilling its contents. We found another bowl called the Waterhole™, but Paul Schmidt the site operator, said that the bowl would spill its contents if rolled or kicked.

We found another website with a pet feeder. This one is the Eat-n-neat™. It holds dry food and is self-dispensing. Suspended it would sustain boat motion. It holds between 10 and 12 pounds of food. It also has a cup that holds water but it would probably spill on a moving boat.

Another option is to build a fitted bracket for the pet bowls that is slightly elevated. Fasten it to a bulkhead leaving enough space under it so that cleanup is easy. Be sure that it is not in a traffic path or in a place where crew will hit it. You can adjust the height to a comfortable level depending upon your pet's size. The very clever wood worker may be able to gimbal a dish, but I don't think your pet really expects you to go that far.

Be sure that you keep bowls and eating areas clean. If you are using a can opener regularly for your food and for your pet's food, remember to wash the cutting blade regularly. In warm climates, the tiny particles of moist food can attract insects and host mold. No one wants possible food poisoning of crew or pet to spoil the cruise.

Pee and Poop

6 The most common question and the biggest concern of owners we meet is how to manage a pet's elimination habits on board a boat. The issue of pee and poop looms regardless of the pet's size, breed, or species. We recognize that the two species are very different. Our experience is that a dog can be trained. With a cat, we only modify or redirect behavior. Therefore, there are two distinct and separate parts in this chapter. If you own a cat, the next part is for you. If you are cruising with a dog, then skip to the second part. If you have both, take notes so that you don't confuse the techniques.

The Cat

Cat owners know how fastidious a cat is. It is typical for a cat to spend 30 minutes at a time licking and cleaning its body. Cats, whether or not they like to swim, want to clean and dry themselves when they emerge from the water. When your cat digs in the litter box, organizes the litter, and then scrapes furiously to cover the deposit, he is responding to instincts and senses. Your cat has a keen sense of smell. Part of his nature, is covering his scent.

In the wild, cats delineate their territory by making deposits as a perimeter telling other cats to stay away. Within its territory, the area that the cat selects for nesting and eating is not where she leaves deposits. Surely from your many hours of cleaning a litter box you know why the cat objects to eating or sleeping near it. Try removing the door or partition that separates your head from your sleeping and eating areas. It is hard to enjoy your food or sleep soundly.

Life with Litter

For a cat to enjoy her existence on a boat there must be provision for peeing and burying deposits that meet with the cat's fastidious approval. A fresh litter box is an easy way to solve the problem. Many of our cruising friends have cats that use the litter box. Those who are liveaboards keep a large supply of litter just as you would in a house. The hard deposits are lifted from the litter with a slotted spoon and taken to the trash or flushed away.

Boat owners who plan to cruise for the weekend or even a month, bring the necessary items—box, scoop, and litter—to the boat. You can always tell who they are because the cat is in her travel bag and the litter pan is on top of the sea bags and bedding. With litter users, we find a 14-pound jug of clumping sand will last about three weeks. Not all of the litter is used in the box because there is always some on the upholstery, the navigation station, and in the sheets if we don't make the bed as soon as we get out of it.

For long term cruising, bluewater voyages included, litter presents some difficulties. Stowing a large quantity of litter takes a fair amount of precious space, and it is heavy. If, however, you depend on buying litter in cruising destinations and foreign countries you might be disappointed. Some cats are fussy about the type or smell of commercial litter products. If you have to buy an unfamiliar brand or something made from an unusual substance, you may find cat deposits in your bed.

One solution for long term voyaging is to use a litter that can be cleaned and recycled. Terry and Mary had two cats that shared a box. On their 36-foot sailboat, space was limited. They had two pans that fit inside one another, the inner one with a perforated bottom. They filled the perforated pan with small river pebbles that could not fall through the holes and set it in the solid pan. After the cats used the pan, the solid matter was lifted out and tossed overboard. The underneath pan was rinsed with salt water. The pebbles in the perforated pan where rinsed clean with salt water and then given a final rinse with fresh water. It proved to be low maintenance and inexpensive. In addition, the cats did not track the pebbles.

Another solution to this problem is to use a course grade of sand in a single pan. Remove the deposits with a slotted spoon. To clean the sand, pour it in a string bag made of fine mosquito netting and drag it in the salt water to clean. Plunging the bag up and down creates a washing action. Rinsing the salt from the sand is important otherwise the sand will hold moisture and smell. Pour about a quart of fresh water slowly over the bag and hang the bag until the sand is dry. This system requires alternating two box-loads of litter. In addition, the periodic addition of new sand keeps the cat happy and entertained as she inspects every new grain. If you are cruising in fresh water, this system is easy and economical.

Tania Aebi had another material for the litterbox. She used sawdust. "Cats can be picky about where they go and nothing is a better substitute than a pile of clean, dry clothes. This was a major bone of contention between us—me trying to keep the litter dry, and he being too picky and not using it regularly. Sometimes, in stormy weather, the box would be brought inside, a condition barely more bearable than smelly clothes, especially when it was sawdust. Apart from maintaining a semblance of dryness, litter quality also had to be addressed and there were different kinds; shavings were best because actual sawdust travels too well. I once made the mistake of getting a bag of teak sawdust and not only did it get tracked everywhere, but the tropical wood bled a rich dark stain that colored the white fiberglass cockpit, adding to the daily chores a new one that involved a lot of scrubbing. The toiletry problem was a considerable one that marred the otherwise perfect relationship, and yet, I put up with it, almost happily."

One other possible pan filler was tested with Pearl. According to Ann, it was a near disaster. "Pearl did very well her first time out; she had the flexibility of a kitten, and we only got as far as the BVIs before turning back to Florida. This time around she's older, and it took longer for her to get comfortable. We spent 4 months winter/spring 2000 in the Bahamas, during which time I used a catbox method that I read about in *Cruising World* our first time out, and which worked very well then. It involves using a square of Astroturf™ instead of kitty litter. Tying a line to the Astroturf™, and to the plastic catbox, and cleaning both in the sea keeps litter out of the thru hulls and off the grocery lists. This time out, she switched to the Astroturf™ without problems—

her own smell was already in the box—but after awhile her box began to smell bad.

"Figuring it was the combination of salt and pee, we tried various non-plastic boxes that were easier to clean. Meanwhile Pearl was getting less happy. She knew the steps we took to start up the engine, and would whine and run when one of us reached for the battery switch. Then she started peeing on a settee cushion, not often, and it seemed to be related to passage making. That summer we sailed to New England, and it wasn't until our return trip in the fall that she began peeing in various spots all over the boat. Everything smelled like Febreze™, the spray we used to get out the pee. Finally she started in on the bed, and that was when I had it.

"It was November and the boat had to be closed up because of the cold. All three of us were frantic by now; she knew she was being "bad" and would get unhappy when she peed, and we were, well, you can imagine for yourselves our state. It was time to take her off the boat and leave her with my parents. She loved the suburbs anyway, the birds and the freedom. But before we did, we gave it one last chance by calling her veterinarian in Annapolis.

"Pearl's own doctor was off having a baby, but the assistant returned our call. ' 'Before the veterinarian goes any further with the problem of Pearl's peeing inappropriately, she wanted me to ask a few questions,' the assistant said. 'First, have there been any changes in Pearl's litter box lately?'

"I was going to say, no, then I stopped myself. Actually we used to use litter, but we have a piece of Astroturf™ now instead." There was silence on the line. "That could be a problem," I said finally.

'Yes, it could. Cats don't like changes in their litter boxes. Even changing litter brands can be a problem. I suggest you buy a five pound bag of kitty litter, and if that doesn't help, call us back.' We did. We threw out the Astroturf™. The smell was better, and Pearl never 'peed inappropriately' again."

Now that you have read about various litter box methods, there is an alternative you can try with your feline cruising friend: the toilet.

Toilet Training Your Cat

The picture illustrates the final objective, and it is a very worthwhile objective by human and feline standards. We pointed out earlier the sensitive nose of a cat. Helping the cat—we didn't say train—learn to use the toilet, frees everyone from smell and litter. There are two books listed in the bibliography that give the specific directions for achieving a litter-less home and boat.

This is the theory as described by Paul Kunkel in *How to Toilet-Train Your Cat:*

"The object is to induce a new form of 'chaining' behavior through progressive modification—gradually altering the environment in which the old behavior was expressed by shifting the height, position, and size of the litter box vis a vis the toilet until box and toilet become one. Unlike conventional training, which is only effective when the animal is paying full attention, progressive modification works no matter what your cat's mood happens to be.

"Each time your cat departs from his previous pattern in response to the next hurdle, following a predetermined path, he establishes a new link in what eventually becomes an entirely new 'chain' of behavior. This 'chaining' phenomenon is a fundamental aspect of feline psychology and the key to the success of the 21-Day Program."

Briefly, the program takes about three weeks of attention on your part. We emphasize your attention because the cat will behave normally if you respond at the opportune moments and don't frighten your cat. Our cat was young for training, which may explain some of his eccentric behavior now. He was box trained immediately as a kitten. In fact, we brought him home from the SPCA, put him in the litter box and he immediately complied with the objective. When he was physically capable of jumping onto bunks, counters, laps, and ladders his toilet training began. We put his litter box next to the toilet in the forward head. We didn't have to tell him where to look, he could smell it. Each day we added newspapers under the litter box to raise it, until the box was at the same height as the toilet seat. When the litter box was even with the toilet, we covered the porcelain bowl of the toilet with plastic wrap as described in Paul Kunkel's *How to Toilet-Train Your Cat.* The cat moved over to the toilet in one try. He

PHOTOGRAPH BY ERIC BROTMAN

Mango switched from a litter box to toilet in three weeks.

was agile and found balance no problem. The litter on the plastic sheet seemed unnecessary because the cat ignored it and simply scratched at the toilet seat and lid then hopped down.

We were over zealous in one area of the training. We encouraged the cat to the extreme. When he hopped on the seat, we would all gather around and tell him how wonderful he was. Three adults squeezed into the forward head must have focused his attention. It took another week to discourage him from waking us at 2 am with happy yowls because he was peeing on the potty. Reading either Kunkel's book or Eric Brotman's *How to Toilet Train Your Cat, the Education of Mango* will help you avoid our mistake. When our cat fell in while we were underway in rough seas, we did have a problem. The trauma caused a type of colitis and the veterinarian advised us to put off retraining for a couple of years.

Mancha was assisted by Dawn and Peter Landon to adjust to a toilet at about the same time as our cat. On a 31-foot boat, it was essential to preserve space. They found that once the cat was well grounded in using a marine toilet, he would use any type of toilet. They traveled by car, stopping with friends or in motels, and each night the cat had his own room, the bathroom. A towel to sleep on, food and water in bowls, and a clean, non-odor producing toilet made it perfect. The cat learned at an early age and managed quite well.

This technique does not work with a tomcat, but as we have indicated earlier, it is essential that cruising pets be neutered or spayed. Multiple cats can adapt to using a single toilet. Once you help your cat to be successful on the toilet, your job is to flush regularly and always put the seat down and leave the lid up.

Whatever methods you select, remember that clean surroundings are essential to a cat's well being. If he is not happy, there will be a mess. Remember, your cat behaves in response to his needs. He is not seeking revenge because that is a human feeling, not cat behavior.

The Dog

Toilet training a dog might be a possibility, but we haven't explored this option. Most dogs are too big to use a litter box although there are some exceptions. Fawna uses a tiny tray with a paper towel for her litter box. However, she only weighs three pounds and eats four ounces of food per day. By contrast, Tristan is a box trained, three-year old, 65-pound standard poodle.

Don Freeman told us the following. "He paper trained himself in a tray made from the lid of a plastic storage box the very first day and has never missed his aim using a tray ever since. The current tray is a large lid from a plastic storage container which has a polypropylene doormat placed on it. The two are tied together at one end and fastened by a line to the boat. He is able to take care of business without wetting his feet and we cast the lot overboard in

Three-pound Fawna can manage with just a paper towel.

PHOTOGRAPH BY JESSIE

return. The only problem he has had using the tray has been when we were being bounced badly. Then he has trouble keeping his balance to perform. Because he was neutered at only three months, he still squats to pee, a great benefit.

Cruising overnight or for the weekend with a dog is quite common. As long as you can take your dog ashore to relieve itself, whether you use a dinghy to go ashore or walk, then training the dog to do something different may require more effort than you want to expend. On the other hand, if you want the dog to be self-sufficient, training may prove valuable.

Modifying Your Life

Over the years, we have seen a variety of methods for dealing with canine elimination. At the top of the list is using artificial turf, a flat of grass, or a heavy-duty piece of cloth as a dog's potty stop. Most of the time a place is selected, the foredeck of both power and sailboats is popular, and covering of some type is placed there for the dog's use. If you have watched your dog over the years, you know that selecting the correct spot is important. If a dog has always used grass, it is likely artificial turf won't have any appeal. Likewise a flat of grass might satisfy a Chihuahua but would hardly be adequate for a German Shepherd. As a puppy, your dog learned it was "bad" to pee and poop on carpets or other fabric so using a tarp or canvas is alien. Another consideration here is the confusion a dog faces if she must learn one place is okay when you are at home, but that same type of place is "bad" or unavailable on the boat. The grass, turf, or cloth will still require cleaning which is a chore.

One of the funniest but workable solutions we saw was in Mexico. We were part of a group of boats anchored along an undeveloped shoreline at Puerto Vallarta called Entrada. Each boat was anchored at the bow and had one or two stern lines running to the shore. One of the boats had a large dog, Neysa, that needed to go ashore twice a day. The owner had a small, hard dinghy on a continuous line from the boat, to shore, and back. When the dog wanted to go ashore, it hopped in the dinghy and waited until the dinghy was pulled to the land. When it had finished romping, sniffing, and unloading, it would climb into the dinghy and wait for the return trip.

This group left their VHF radios on during the morning to make and receive calls about shopping trips, weather, and social events. One morning, we noticed that the dog had gone to shore then returned to the dinghy, but had not been pulled back to the boat. It was turning around, standing, then sitting, but not getting anyone's attention. Being well behaved, it didn't bark. I picked up the microphone and said in a sad voice, "I'm in the dinghy." Seconds later everyone was on deck and giggling as the sheepish owner came into his cockpit and pulled the dog and dinghy back to the boat. The system does work if you are close to shore, the beach is uninhabited, and you don't forget the dog.

Training Your Dog

Recently, we talked to dog owners who had successfully trained their pets to pee and poop on the boat. Ann and Mike McDougall who own Boris, the giant Schnauzer, cruise with him on a 47' sailboat. Boris has been trained to do his business on command. He hears the command "Go for a walk," walks to the foredeck, and relieves himself. Training began on a leash and Ann said that she walked him around and around until he could not wait any longer. Now he doesn't need a leash or companion.

Boris has also participated in training other dogs. By invitation, Boris comes aboard a boat that has an untrained dog, and leaves a deposit. The dog on the boat responds by covering up Boris' scent and overcomes at the same time whatever inhibitions had existed. This visit from Boris has not been the total training. However, the owners of the dogs in training have said that Boris' gift has made deck pooping acceptable, and their dogs have progressed.

Several years ago, Dr. Marjorie L. Smith wrote a treatise entitled *You Can Teach Your Dog to Eliminate on Command.* It had been out of print for sometime, but you will find the new listing in the bibliography. The basic

The odors from another dog can motivate your dog to poop and pee on board.

information is simple and straightforward. It does require an owner to understand the training process and be capable of spending time with the dog for at least a week. Once the dog has been trained then other handlers can manage the dog with minimal fuss.

The following is a very brief summary of Dr. Smith's technique. It takes time and patience but training your dog so that he can live comfortably aboard the boat with a minimum of fuss for you is a huge reward.

The basics of the program require recognizing when your dog needs to pee or poop. The typical pattern with most dogs on a leash is to sniff the ground, walk around in circles, assume the normal position for his size and sex, contract the necessary muscles, and do the doo. Smith describes this process with sketches. According to her program, the key is to have selected a very specific phrase, one easily heard and recognized by the dog. Just as the dog opens the sphincter muscle, this code phrase is spoken softly several times. Based on work originally developed by Pavlov, this process causes the dog to associate the phrase with the activity. The repetition of this phrase at the precise moment is, according to Dr. Smith, the learning opportunity for the dog. As soon as elimination has begun, it is important to stop using this phrase, and switch to a brief word of praise. In addition, nothing should be said as the activity ends. After the dog has been conditioned, typically accomplished in a week's time, you should be able to use the phrase to trigger the response. Living and cruising with a dog trained to PPC will simplify your life. Your dog will know your expectations making his life simpler.

Trained cats and dogs offer you a new kind of freedom when you go cruising. After years aboard and miles of water, we can only hope that you will try the appropriate training. The rewards are worth the effort.

Pet Etiquette

7 Etiquette describes a standard of behavior that makes it possible to exist as a member of a community without offending other members. It sounds daunting when we use this term to describe the behavior of a dog or cat. Actually, it is a matter of survival for the pet in question and acceptance for the pet owner. The cruising community is small and close. When a breach of etiquette occurs, everyone knows about it. While we expect the unique and unusual among new cultures, we don't forgive bad manners among our own. Learning how to be welcome with your pet in the cruising community requires study and effort.

Cat Etiquette

We began life with our second boat-cat by spending a week traveling in a van. We were afraid of losing him in a strange place so we put him into a harness and on a leash immediately. He grew up thinking this regalia was part of his normal existence. We grew with him learning that we could take him off the boat, walk him on the dock, and enjoy some freedom knowing he wasn't a nuisance.

There are "cat people" who will tell you that it is cruel and unfair to leash train a cat. This permissive attitude assumes that it is acceptable for your feline to go anywhere he wants, which is a recipe for disaster. In the cruising community, keeping your cat aboard is plain, good manners. For those still in doubt, the leash is also a way to guarantee that your cat doesn't wander into the territory of feral cats and almost certain death. Feral cats are not usually neutered, they are tough and fierce, and unfortunately carry a variety of diseases and parasites.

The most serious transgression where cruising cats are concerned is roaming. Some people are terrified of all felines. There are those who are extremely allergic to cats. There are those who don't want animal scents left by a wandering cat as it will invite other animals to investigate. Many simply don't want uninvited two-footed or four-footed visitors. Regardless of the reasons, you must not allow your cat to wander off your boat.

Unfortunately, cat-lovers who cruise, but don't have cats, can be your worst enemy. They tell you, "I love cats. Your cat can come aboard my boat anytime." They will entice your cat with treats and attention. Your cat cannot distinguish between those who like cats and those who don't. You must ask the cat enthusiast to cease and desist. I always tell them that if they need a "cat-fix" that they are welcome to come over and visit our cat, on our boat. Usually they don't take me up on the offer more than once or twice. Our cat is friendly but always shows affection to the family and ignores visitors. After that, the cat-lover seems to accept the situation and our cat is no longer the center of unwanted attention.

Leash Training Your Cat

In an earlier chapter, we mentioned that the best-adjusted cruising cat is one that lives aboard from early kittenhood. Leash training is also best done from the very beginning. Even when your kitten is too small to climb out of the cabin and can't wander, put a harness on her. It is important to put a harness on your kitten as early as possible. Finding a small harness can be a challenge. The soft, cloth strap-harness can be tightened by sewing tucks into the straps. Release the tucks as the cat grows. If your cat wears a flea collar, be sure that the harness is separate from the collar. Once we put the harness on the kitten, we leave it there more-or-less permanently. Removing a harness because it is bedtime or you think it is a good break tells the cat that it can come off. It seems to challenge the curious nature of a cat. As the cat matures, we occasionally remove it, but not as a regular routine. The harness may save your cat's life if you have to retrieve her from the water. The harness gives you a claw-proof handle to retrieve your cat from wet or dangerous situations.

Attaching the leash can create a game or havoc. I like to let the kitten drag the leash around so that it becomes familiar and ceases to be interesting. A short piece of line without knots or loops that catch corners and equipment is a good starter leash. A regular leash is too much for a kitten to drag around and it could create problems.

The first time you try stopping the kitten's forward progress is always a surprise. Hold the end of the leash when the kitten is still and let him take a step or two. Then tug the leash so the kitten has to stop. He will pull and turn around to exam the problem. When the kitten relaxes and moves again, tug him to a stop. If the kitten starts to run, don't jerk him off his feet. It is better to let him romp and play with the leash than get stunned or hurt by a sudden pull.

As the cat acclimates to the leash—please note we don't say trained—take the end in hand and follow where the cat leads. The cat will be aware of your presence but if you let her wander, she won't be threatened by your presence. After you and the cat acclimate to the teamwork, you can stop her

PHOTOGRAPH BY JESSIE

Even cats can learn to walk on a leash.

gently and pull in a direction of your choice. If the cat doesn't cooperate, pick her up and put her where you want her to be.

Taking the cat for a walk in the same manner you would walk a dog requires lots of training time on your part. "Heel," "sit," and commands of that sort won't register with most cats. Persuading the cat to accept the leash as a control is not difficult but requires diligence. The training will allow you to keep the cat in a specific place without holding her or locking her up.

When the boat is underway or at anchor away from other boats, our cat wanders without a leash because he cannot trespass on other boats or property without a swim. If we are rafted-up or on a dock, the cat goes on deck with supervision or on a leash until we are certain that he will stay aboard. Even after months of good behavior, our cat will occasionally test going ashore or onto someone's boat, and he is quickly returned, put below, and admonished for his behavior. He then goes back on a leash when on deck.

We aren't the only cat-owning cruisers who learned the value of harness and leash for a feline. This is what Ann had to say about their cat. "Pearl is a ten-year old gray medium short-haired cat we brought home from the pound in Melbourne, Florida as a kitten to our first cruising boat. She lived aboard with us for a year and a half, then at various times we all lived on boats on the hard, or traveled, or lived in houses. She wears a purple harness all the time, and we'd take her for walks on a leash whenever she went by car. She'd love highway rest stops, and always seemed to know where the pet walking stations were. People thought she was a dog."

Our biggest mistake in training has always been consistency. It is unfair to expect the cat to read your mind. Doing something the same way, every time gives your cat a chance to recognize the situation and the expected behavior.

Marking

Cats are notorious for marking territory. They constantly rub against objects including owners, to mark them with their scent. On boats, uncontrolled cats will mark boats by urinating or defecating. This is not acceptable to anyone. First, the odor is nearly impossible to remove from sail bags, canvas covers, or wood. Even if you scrub with strong chemicals, the odor lingers and is discernable by the trespassing cat and other cats. We've gone as far as throwing away sail bags and getting new ones when strays have marked our boat.

If your cat is a guilty party, it is reasonable for the victim to expect restitution for the damage your pet did. It is a hazard of cat ownership that you need to consider. When others know that you control your pet and keep her aboard, they are less likely to accuse her of something that a stray or feral cat may have done.

Biting

Some cats develop a habit of biting. We learned from our own mistakes where biting was concerned. As a kitten, we let him assume hands and fingers were toys. We tickled him or poked him and he would attack. Unfortunately, this behavior continued into adulthood. With another cat, we used toys for play. The difference is significant. Toys offered the opportunity for exercise and we didn't bleed from zealous attacks.

We do get nibbles from the cat. Little nibbles and noises display interest and attention in us. Sometimes the cat wants attention, and a nibble on a finger, toe, or ear is a way of saying, "I'm here."

Strays

One night in Japan, we returned to the boat after dinner to discover our cat was entertaining a local cat. They were seated on opposite sides of the dinghy. There were no signs of fighting or animosity of any kind. Our arrival caused the guest to depart suddenly. Our cat gave us a quiet comment and went below.

Later that night our cat wakened us crashing back and forth through the boat. When we turned on the light, we discovered he was chasing a small mouse. As the cat raced up the companionway ladder with us in hot pursuit, we saw the stray from the earlier visit up on the dock. We assumed that she had brought the mouse as a gift, as it could not have gotten on the boat except to be carried or dropped on the deck.

We tried to look at this experience as a cultural event. The Japanese people were the most hospitable we have ever encountered, constantly plying us with food and gifts. We can only assume that their cats have adopted behavior that appears the same.

Don't allow strays to come aboard of their own accord and don't pick up strays and bring them aboard. Encouraging strays to come aboard by offering food exposes your cat to disease and parasites. Discourage all contact with strays.

Dog Etiquette

Canines seem to understand the value of relating positively to people or at least one person. They bond in obvious ways and adjust their behavior. Their natural pack instinct makes training a way for them to learn where they fit in the hierarchy of your pack. Training them to be well mannered is easier than training felines but training is often neglected because of ignorance or laziness.

Dogs, like cats, must obey certain rules because there are cruisers who don't want them aboard, who are afraid of them, who are allergic to them, or simply don't like them. You may have security as a motive for keeping a dog aboard and train her for that purpose. However, you must remember that you are liable for your dog's behavior. Dogs that bite are not welcome anywhere.

Obedience Training

A few simple commands that your dog will respond to immediately will make your life much easier. "Come, sit, stay," and "heel" are a good beginning for any dog. If you can't train your dog or can't get the results you want, it will be worth your while to get a professional to help you. Practice with the dog regularly to insure continued good behavior. Even with training, allowing your dog to run free is no more acceptable than it is for a cat.

Your dog should wear a collar and leash whenever you go ashore. The very best behaved dog may misbehave because of unusual sights and sounds in a strange locale. Chickens fighting or running loose in the street, large, four-footed animals used as transportation, or sudden, loud noises from ancient motors conspire to undo the toughest training. If you don't need to take your animal ashore into populated areas, you may find it easier on you and your pet's psyche to keep your dog aboard.

As we indicated earlier, obedience training is essential to the success of training your dog to eliminate on command. Using the leash and your specific vocabulary makes this training an easier process.

Marking

Dogs expect to mark territory. Usually, urinating over another dog's scent is typical behavior. On your own boat, your dog will have marked the territory to declare ownership. If you take your dog aboard another vessel or on shore, your dog will do likewise. Except in the case where your dog has been invited aboard to expedite the toilet training process, marking another boat is not acceptable. It is better to leave your pet aboard your boat when you socialize. If you want your dog to socialize or exercise with other cruisers' dogs, organize a trip ashore to a specified location away from non-pet owners.

Barking

Many cruisers have dogs aboard for companionship and security. A watchdog on shore uses barking to sound the alarm. Just as a neighbor's barking dog is a nuisance to the neighborhood, having a neighboring boat with a barking dog is unpleasant. Loud noises carry a long distance over the water. Uncontrolled barking is not acceptable in an anchorage or marina even when the owner declares it is security. Neighbors will have little sympathy for your need for a sense of security if they can't get any peace and quiet.

Some dogs have been bred for specific purposes and barking is part of the breeding. However, the nervous dog, the fearful dog, the dog without confidence is likely to be a habitual barker. Once he starts, he is hard to stop.

The sensitive hearing typical in most dogs permits the dog to hear sounds that you don't hear. A normal response from a dog is to bark when he hears an unknown sound. As a cruiser, you cannot permit your dog to bark constantly. Training the dog is essential. If you cannot keep your dog quiet, especially at night, then using a muzzle or keeping the dog below may be the only way to manage. In fact, security dogs are often kept below at night because they create a genuine surprise should there be an uninvited guest.

Cruisers often live in very close proximity to one another. A crowded anchorage is likely to cause nervous and untrained dogs to bark constantly. If your dog is not a barker, beware of letting him pick up the bad habits of dogs in an anchorage. If someone else's dog persists in barking, you will need to speak to them. Ask them to consider putting the dog below decks. There are occasions when the pack instinct to howl will take over. The best you can do is to bring your dog below. Suggest to other dog owners that they do the same to break the cycle. It is neither unfair nor inappropriate for your fellow cruisers to expect peace and tranquility.

Strays

Most dog owners know that feral dogs can be a serious problem. Strays in foreign countries are frequently feral and must be avoided. Sometimes it appears that countries have rigorous restrictions on pet importation yet allow local dogs to roam.

Diseased strays are a serious threat to the health of your dog. Taking pity and feeding or providing water for a stray is not a good idea. If you become a "regular stop" on a stray's itinerary, it will be difficult to rid yourself of the responsibility the dog believes you have assumed.

In Mexico, a lovely mongrel adopted Jim. Each day when we landed the dinghy on the beach, she was waiting for us. She followed us faithfully on all our errands. One night she followed us into a restaurant. The owner assumed the dog was ours, and although he didn't permit pets, he allowed the dog to follow us to keep our patronage. When he finally asked about the dog, Jim explained that she had simply followed us everywhere and we had no idea who owned her. The owner immediately removed the dog from the premises, and he was not very happy with us. We should have discouraged the dog from following us around, but it seemed so clever that she could identify Jim each day and liked to follow him. Although we never fed her or encouraged her, we didn't discourage her either. It was our mistake.

In Japan, a similar situation developed when Jim was carrying water in jerry cans from a nearby faucet across the road to our boat. The tap dripped between trips and a very thirsty dog took advantage of the puddle that developed on the cement pad below the faucet. After the chore was complete, the dog flopped down on the edge of the road. Every time Jim came into the cockpit, the dog raised his head. If we left the boat, the dog trotted obediently at our heels. We tried to get him to go away but he persisted. One night, he followed us into a different neighborhood where we went into a restaurant. When we left the restaurant, the dog was gone and we did not see him again.

Something as simple as stopping to pet a cute stray while you are ashore could bring the gift of fleas back to the boat and your dog. More serious would be contact between a stray and your dog. Parasites and disease from a feral dog could harm your dog and you.

Feral dogs are frequently vicious, particularly in a group. Attempting to befriend these dogs, as harmless or hungry as they appear, puts you at risk. Your instinct to help an animal in these circumstances is admirable but reason must prevail for your sake and the sake of others.

People Etiquette

We have discussed good manners for the cats and the dogs. There are a couple of words for owners of those four-footed friends.

Taking your animal into town on a leash is a decision to think through carefully. Taking your animal, leashed or not, is not your right when you visit another cruiser's boat. Assuming that everyone will appreciate, Fido or Felix is a serious mistake. If you are enroute to or from another destination and stop to visit a boat, leave your pet in the dinghy. The situation should not force the owners or crew of the boat to feel any obligation to entertain your pet.

Provide a comfortable, protected place for your pet in your dinghy. Be sure to keep the visit short so that neither your host nor your pet becomes agitated. If someone insists on having your pet come aboard, that can become a problem for you. You have trained your dog or cat to stay on your boat. Your hospitable friends should understand this explanation and not be offended. Allowing her to be on another boat will confuse her training. Explain that you really cannot bring the pet aboard, but if they would like to offer her a drink of water, you will give it to your dog or cat in the dinghy.

We had a group of people on our boat one evening to chat and have a drink. A guest insisted on holding our cat on his lap. The cat, like many, was not fond of being cuddled by strangers. The situation finally erupted into a struggle and I tried to remove the cat. The guest was not going to give in and everyone else was becoming upset. I finally snatched the cat from his lap and put him into our aft cabin. Everyone seemed relieved, but during the rest of the evening, I had to stop our guest from going in search of the cat.

The guest's behavior was childish. It was embarrassing and he did not come to visit again. The smart thing on my part would have been to put the cat into the aft cabin before our guests arrived.

It may seem that restricting your dog or cat from visiting other boats is severe. However, you have an obligation to your fellow cruisers and to your pet. If you are cruising, protect your pets and protect your friendships.

Kennel Training

8 Your pet has a place at home that it regards as "home." Whether you spend brief periods on your boat or live aboard, your pet needs a "home" on the boat. Cats and dogs approach this issue differently, and have different requirements. Regardless, they share the need for a place of their own.

Dogs

Doghouses, dog beds, or crates are acceptable as homes for most dogs. For the outdoor dog, a house that allows him to come and go, day or night, is quite a good arrangement. The dog that is a companion dog finds the isolation of an outdoor house a scary place. When you think about having a home on the boat, your pet's usual patterns need to be considered. Your dog needs the security of knowing there is a special place that is his. In addition, that place must be comfortable, safe, and clean.

The companion dog will be happy with any place close to you. As long you are within earshot, the security of closeness will make the chosen place acceptable. The outdoor dog that you take to the boat may have just the opposite reaction. Dogs, outdoor or companion, are happiest with human contact. However, the condition of confinement that the boat imposes on an outdoor dog can be frustrating. Running, coming and going at will, and chasing wildlife, are not practical activities on a boat. If you take your dog on your boat, it will be your responsibility to provide an environment that satisfies your dog's expectations and experience.

A dog that has had kennel training since puppyhood is much more cooperative about accepting a new "home" on your boat. Teaching your dog about a crate or bed as his place should begin early. Sending your dog to his "room" or "bed" allows you to put your dog in a specific place.

As a puppy, Tyler learned to "kennel up." Going to a specific location on command was part of his normal routine. If he was expected to go to sleep or for some reason was to be separated from his owner for a time, he was sent to his place. If he was told "kennel up" as punishment, putting a towel over the door of the crate differentiated it from the usual place. As the puppy progressed, he would kennel up with the door left open. The next step was to kennel up, leave the door open, and then his owners left the boat. If he left the crate and chewed on items, he was sent back to kennel up with a towel over the door. When he had successfully passed the test and didn't chew anything while alone, he was rewarded. Each time his owners returned or released him from the crate, he was given a happy greeting.

There is some disagreement about using this place for discipline as exile creates a sense of punishment. If your dog makes a bad association with a place designed for her protection, using it may confuse your pet. Your dog needs to be trained that going to her "room" or "bed" is a positive routine. For Tyler the difference was the towel over the door, creating a specific isolation.

A crate or carrier used for travel creates a specific place. Your dog sees the kennel as routine and has learned that motion is normal when the crate is in the car. Making the transfer from car travel to boat travel will be positive if trips in the carrier in the car have been positive. If trips to the veterinarian are the only time the crate is used, it may have negative associations that you will need to correct. A few trips to the park or a drive-through restaurant where your dog shares a small treat will help erase bad associations. Once the crate is a good place for your dog to kennel up, use the crate aboard the boat.

Staying in the kennel is normal. Select the location of your dog's crate very carefully. No matter how comfortable the bed or carrier, if you put it in the wrong place, your pet will be unhappy. Left to his own devices, a dog will find a place that accommodates his size, has a minimum of motion and noise, the temperature is comfortable, is less likely to be stepped on, and your presence is assured. You need to use the same guidelines when choosing a location for the crate on your boat.

Boats are designed to be lighter in the ends. These areas give the boat buoyancy and the motion is exaggerated. Likewise, the higher you are from the water on a boat, the more extreme the motion. The center of gravity is usually just below the water line and sustains the least motion. Ideally, you want to locate your dog's place where there is the least motion. Unfortunately, on larger powerboats, the place of least motion will be the engine room. The next best place would be just aft of the engine room if there is cabin space.

The other determining factors are space, temperature, and your proximity. If there is no living space below the waterline aft of the engine, you need to find the next best location as close to the center of the boat as possible. Remember what we said earlier about the noise from the engine. Your dog's sensitive hearing will eliminate being too close to the engine. Look for that spot that offers the least motion and protects your pet's hearing. Be sure there is adequate space for a crate or bed that accommodates your dog comfortably. This spot must have good air circulation. You may need to add a small fan to keep air circulating.

PHOTOGRAPH BY JESSIE

A bed in your pilot house keeps your dog close and comfortable.

If your dog pants constantly in the location find a way to make it cooler. Secure the bed or crate so that it will not shift if conditions become rolly. And finally, make sure your dog is not isolated from you. If you can be heard, or better yet seen, your dog will feel secure when told to "kennel up," "go to your room," or whatever command you devise.

If you expect to run only in daylight hours and sleep at night, the special place for sleeping does not need to be as motion-proof. However, you will need to have a location for daylight running where your dog can rest comfortably. Our neighbor Andrew Fraser's Nordhaven has stabilizers and flopper-stoppers reducing the motion, which makes the pilothouse very tenable for Murray when the boat is underway.

On a sailboat, the point of sail changes and the degree of motion changes accordingly. Going to weather has the most amount of motion while broad reaching seems to have the least amount of motion. Some cruisers who sail downwind with a double head rig experience extremely rolly rides. This is unnecessary and improving your sailing skills will make you and your dog happier. In general, locations aft of the mast or mast support post below decks will have the least motion.

Improvising a kennel on board is important with a big dog.

In our cutter-rigged, 48' sloop, the distance halfway between the mast and the transom is the easiest ride.

Tyler is a big dog. Using a crate on board the boat proved impractical. It occupies too much floor space in the main salon of the Passport 40. To continue his training without confusing him about "kennel up," the area under the dinette table is his place. The blanket on the floor and his favorite chew toy make it clear to all this is Tyler's place. He has easy access to the aft-of-mast location, there is good air circulation, and he can stretch out comfortably or sit upright. Best of all, he can see and hear Dan and Chris from this spot whether they are below or on deck.

The kennel or bed that belongs to your dog must be clean. Remove soiled items, air cushions and blankets, sweep or mop regularly to remove hair and dirt. Keep food and water away from this area to eliminate accidental messes from spillage. Check when cleaning that nothing in the surrounding area will create a hazard by falling into or against the area. If you are using a crate or bed, check the fastenings to insure it won't slip or slide while the boat is underway. This is especially important on a sailboat where the heeling motion sends things tumbling.

Cats

Cat requirements are similar yet quite different from dog requirements when it comes to having a "place." First, don't expect to train your cat to "kennel up." You may decide to put your cat in the aft cabin, or close it up in the head, but it is unlikely to go voluntarily to a designated spot on your command. You can cooperatively arrange acceptable locations for your cat.

The cat carrier used for trips to the veterinarian carries the same onus for cats as it does for dogs. The negative association of shots with the carrier needs to be overcome if you plan to use it on the boat. As with a dog, cat owners need to take the cat in her carrier for good experiences. Our cat loves to investigate bags and packages from shopping tours. Taking him out of the carrier while the car is parked allows time for thorough investigation of our cargo. Leaving the carrier open at home or on the boat, permits your cat to choose it as a location. Most cats are curious and suspicious. They will spend many minutes checking an item before determining whether it is of interest to them. If your cat voluntarily crawls inside and curls up for a nap, the carrier has passed inspection. However, it is useless to assume that the carrier will be the only designated place your cat occupies. Curiosity is never totally satisfied.

Many cats like the coziness of the carrier. Nevertheless, the arrival of a box or basket creates the need for your cat to examine it and determine its value. An empty box brought aboard may become a new "place" for your cat because it is new. After a day or two, the box, like a new toy, is ignored. Cats develop habitual places but we can't assume that they will always be the first choice.

Likewise, the cozy carrier may be great when it's cool but unacceptable when it is warm. If you are cruising from a cool climate to a warm one, heat will be a

Cats like spaces where they can spy on others and not be seen.

major factor in your cat's selection of the right place. It may suddenly decide to sleep on the cool sole boards in the head rather than on carpeting. It may decide to sleep on its back in an open location with all four paws in the air. It may crawl into whatever dark, cool space is available.

If the reverse is true of the weather, you may find the cat will want to share your body heat. Halifax decided to sleep inside the bottom of Alvah's mummy bag. We've spent more than one night wrestling with our cat pushing to get in between us for warmth. Getting up from a cushion on a cool morning means you have surrendered it to the cat. The cat wants to absorb the body heat you left behind.

The nocturnal habits of a cat have much to do with where she decides to kennel up. At night, a cat is often bright-eyed and alert. In the wild, cats typically prowl looking for small nocturnal prey. One night we had our bunk, pillows, and inert bodies covered with large black moths caught as they fluttered about our anchor light. Beyond filling his stomach, Boca showed his feline acumen as a hunter. Years later, we still found moth body parts under sole boards, in the bilge, and in far corners of deck level lockers. Fortunately, night hunting has ceased.

Not all cats prowl at night. Not all cats are willing to endure cold or wind. All cats will determine where they are most comfortable. If there are places that are dangerous for your cat, then those must be made inaccessible. This is like putting toddler fences at your stairway. In fact, you must be wary of places your cat can creep into at night, and those from which she can escape.

We have a vent at the transom. The cowl was broken and we couldn't find a replacement. We decided to leave the vent partially covered with the damaged cowl to keep air circulating through the boat. One night we heard a terrible ruckus in the cockpit. The cat had found its way out the vent and onto a strange dock. He is very quick and made it back through the vent to safety, before a huge Maine Coon cat caught up with him.

Try to arrange appealing spots for your cat. A cardboard box with shredded paper is a great toy and resting-place. A beehive basket with a peephole allows your cat to see yet be undetected. An oversized pillow big enough to accommodate the entire body of your cat even when it stretches is a good idea. With a kitten scale things down to create coziness until it is ready to venture out. Live aboard cats are inclined to be more sociable because you are together in a confined space. You may find your cat expects to share your space—your bed, your cushion, your lap. Your cruising friend may prove to be more aware and dependent on you than you expect.

Regardless of the variety of spaces your cat uses, it is important that it has a space of its own. If it likes the cat carrier or basket, keep that place clean and available to your cat. Be sure to wash any bedding, and keep the area free from food and other organic matter.

In rough weather, your cat may hide. It may take some time to discover that hiding place, but the cat will stay put as long as he is fearful. If you try to remove your cat from his protection, be prepared for a struggle. As soon as the cat has a chance, he will hide again. If you notice, your cat's choice of hiding place will be comfortable and quiet. He will seek a place with the least motion and noise. Once you know the pattern and place, accept your cat's choice. If you can make it more comfortable or safer, do so.

Some cruisers put cats into the carrier assuming that it is the safest spot in rough weather. Forcing your cat to be in a place where she isn't comfortable can result in a very sick and frightened pet. If you think the carrier is necessary, put it in the place your cat selects. A cat carrier up on a bunk or dinette subjects its tenant to unnecessary motion. That same carrier under a bunk or behind a companionway ladder sustains less motion and is a safer place for your cat.

If your cat disappears within the confines of the boat when the weather isn't rough, be sure to check her for symptoms of illness. She may simply have chosen a new place to rest, but cats frequently crawl into hiding spots when they are sick.

Pet Fashions for Cruising

9 I am certain that I am not the only person to giggle at the array of pet fashions available in the pet supply store. At the same time, I must admit that the inventiveness of some items is amazing and very practical. Just as you need specialized gear for life on the water, your pet should have some items before going cruising.

PFD's

The pet personal flotation device, PFD, is essential. Your pet may not enjoy wearing it any more than a small child does. PFD's are cumbersome and not especially comfortable. They inhibit natural motion for some cats and dogs, so wearing them is not a happy experience. Unfortunately, I think this is one of those times when safety outweighs the comfort factor and your pet will have to endure.

The variety of PFD's on the market is awesome. I saw a small one that was decorated to look like a tuxedo, too cute. Most of them are not extreme, but apparently style is an issue for some cruisers looking for pet PFD's. Of all the possible characteristics important in PFD selection, fashion is the least important.

First, the device should be highly visible. If your dog or cat has fallen overboard, a bright yellow or orange object bobbing along in the water is much more visible than colors that blend in—blue, green, gray, tan. It does not matter what you think your pet likes since cats and dogs cannot distinguish color. If you don't like the color, you may have to reconsider how important your pet's life is to you. If you look at safety gear in the marine stores, you will see that the USCG approved people-gear is typically yellow or orange. High visibility makes rescue easier and faster. Follow that same guideline when buying a PFD for your pet. Reflective tape on the PFD might improve the visibility of a darker one you already own. It can also help if you have to retrieve your pet from water at night.

Second, the device must fit snuggly. If your cat or dog can wriggle out of the PFD, it will be useless. Cats in particular are clever at getting out of gear, so you need to be sure it fits. You can take your dog to the store for fitting. This allows you to discover any difficulties in dressing your dog as well as finding a close fitting PFD. If you order a PFD via the Internet, make sure you can return it if it doesn't fit properly. Taking cats to the store may not be as practical. So make sure the store will let you exchange the PFD in the event the one you select doesn't fit your cat.

Most flotation is designed with straps that can be fitted around the body. Some vests have narrow straps that may cut into your pet's stomach. If you have a large dog, over a hundred pounds, look for very sturdy stitching, straps more than an inch wide, and plenty of flotation. Make sure your pet can move and sit comfortably wearing the vest. The styles with three straps, one around the front of the chest and two under the body, offer more security as your pet cannot slip out.

Third, look for a handle on the top of the PFD. When you need to lift your pet from the water, this handle will make it easy. When attempting a rescue from a boat, boat motion splashes water making it difficult to get near to your swimming pet. Using a sturdy boat hook, thread it through the handle to bring your pet alongside then lift it from the water. For a large dog, the PFD strap can be threaded with a halyard from the hoist or mast to make it easier to lift.

Fourth, there needs to be adequate buoyancy for the size of your pet. The flotation in the vest should raise the head, shoulders, and back above the water. When your pet is in ordinary swimming mode—testing this is a challenge—usually the head is above the water. On some bigger dogs, they will display some of the shoulder area. Remember, if your pet is in rough water, the buoyancy will be critical for keeping his head above water.

Be sure to check the BoatUS website listed in the appendix for information about various types of PFD's that have been tested. In the November 2000 test, the device that seemed to be the choice of the participants was the K9 Dog Float Coat™ from Ruff Wear. The float coat wraps around the dog and does not have webbing straps under the body. The colors are yellow or red, and the coat has reflective tape stripes as well. The size range will accommodate cats up through extra-large dogs. The one dog that couldn't be fitted with this particular device was a corgi. The K9 Float Coat™ was also the most expensive of the flotation devices that I inspected. The prices—based on size—range from $39.95 to $74.95. You will find their website in the appendix.

Two other companies listed in the website appendix had PFD's that warrant consideration. Neither of these companies was included in the BoatUS testing.

The Neo Paw™ makes a pet PFD that has a unique feature. It has a removable chest piece that is "Y" shaped. It fastens to the body strap and across the chest to either side. This provides additional buoyancy for your pet. The nylon webbing is wider than one inch. Made in Canada, this brand was not available in the larger marine stores. I found one in a pet boutique the manufacturer had listed on the Internet. That website is in the appendix. Prices ranged from $26 for extra small to $46 for the XX large.

Spending on good gear should include your pet's PFD.

PHOTOGRAPH BY RUFFWEAR

The Crewsaver Company has been making life saving devices since 1936. Their "Petfloat" is highly regarded by marine safety expert, Henry Marx of Landfall Navigation in Greenwich, Connecticut. Its strength is soft foam as opposed to the rigid foam found in some of the other models. Additionally, it has a padded chest strap, uses reflective tape, and offers an identification placket.

Some advertisements and labels imply that the devices are USCG approved. There are no standards for pet flotation devices. However, there are materials that the USCG approves for flotation devices and those materials may be used in the various pet PFD's on the market.

If you are just starting out in boats, purchasing a less expensive PFD for your pet is probably a good idea. However, if you discover that long term boating or voyaging is what you want to do, purchase the best equipment available for yourself, your family, and your pet.

Harnesses

Pet supply stores offer a variety of harnesses for cats and dogs. The marine environment is hard on certain materials and those materials should be avoided in your pet's boat wardrobe. Leather tends to mildew and ultimately rot from moisture. If you ordinarily use a leather harness, I would recommend buying one made of fabric webbing that you can rinse and easily maintain. Another advantage of the cloth

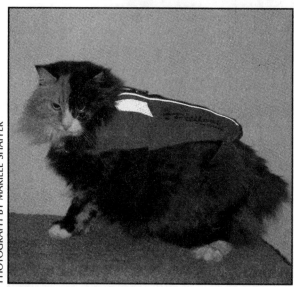

PHOTOGRAPH BY MARILEE SHAFFER

webbing is that you can sew it if you need to customize the harness to your pet's body.

In the saltwater environment, most metal fastenings on pet harnesses will rust. A harness with brass or stainless steel fittings would be ideal. Check the rivets, D rings,

The British Crewsaver has an ID packet sewn in.

and closures. We found harnesses with plastic closing devices that don't rust. However, be alert because the plastic will become brittle with time and will break easily.

Harness designs seem to be of two types. One design is the figure eight with a loop for the head, the crossover on the top of the shoulders, and the closure under the chest behind the front legs. The D ring for a leash is placed at the crossover point. The second design is similar to a cage. One strap encircles the head below the neck, and a second strap encircles the chest behind the front legs. The two straps are joined on the pet's back by a short length of material, and joined underneath, between the legs by another piece of material. The strap around the chest has a closure. A D ring is attached at the base of the top connector strap to fasten a leash.

We have tried both designs on our cat. The cage style harness fits our cat better, and it fits snugly. Our cat is a cousin of Harry Houdini, and has little problem escaping from harnesses. We have learned his technique and switched to the cage model simply because we can usually catch him in mid-attempt. Typically in escaping a harness, cats will face the direction of the leash or restraint and pull back. The figure eight design fails at this point, as the chest strap pulls away. The cat then lowers its head and pulls again slipping the crossover point over its ears. The cage design with the attaching straps on top and bottom requires the cat to remove its legs, one at a time, from the chest strap.

If you have an open boat and insufficient space for a crate or carrier, you might consider the VestHarness™. It restrains an animal while protecting it from sudden stops. The bouncing motion in an open boat or sudden stops can injure your pet. Typically used in conjunction with a car seat belt, adapting it for use in your open boat will give you peace of mind and keep your pet safe in the open. The website is in the appendix.

Always look for a good fit in a harness. Avoid a harness that tightens around the neck. If you have to lift your pet in an emergency, the harness shouldn't put stress on your pet's neck or throat. A collar used for restraint is not safe for lifting your pet.

Boots

Boots for your pet may seem outlandish, but given earlier comments on deck surfaces, you might want to consider them. The only brand of boots we have seen in use are the Bark n' Boots™ . There is another company, Neo Paws™, that manufactures three types of shoes called Neo Paws™.

The selling point with both companies is protection for your pet's feet, and additionally, protection for your floors, decks, upholstery, etc. Just like deck shoes and boots for humans, the issue of traction is important.

Boots for your dog offer traction and deck protection.

We did encounter some debate about the flexibility of the soles. Leather soles have been used on some models of dog shoe but they do not wear well. There is a problem with mold in a damp environment, too. The Neo Paws™ regular shoe has a treaded rubber sole. Their high performance shoe construction features a formed and molded rubber sole that covers the entire paw area. Their summer shoe has a double mesh upper and the regular rubber sole. The regular boots range from XS to XXL with prices from $30 to $38. The High Performance boot has a size range from S to XXXL with prices ranging from $52 to $68. The summer model has a similar size and price range.

The Bark n' Boots™ are made in one style. The soles are made of a special material called Reprotek, which is described as "high mileage and having a grippy surface." They have added a heavy-duty nylon material to reinforce the toe area for durability. Their boots range from XS to XXL. All sizes cost $38.00

One of the main selling points for both Bark n' Boots™ and Neo Paws™, is that they stay on your dog's foot. The only dog we know that wears deck boots is the Golden Retriever Chaucer. Karen says that each time she puts them on Chaucer, he needs a moment or two to adjust. He walks a few steps and is quickly loping along the dock with all four paws covered.

Successfully dressing your dog in boots seems to be a matter of practice. The manufactures recommend trimming your dog's toenails for comfort. Comfort and fit are issues to consider. If clipping nails is enough protection for your boat and your dog is able to stay upright on deck, you may not want to consider boots.

The only disadvantage in expecting your dog to wear boots on the boat is climate. Just as we enjoy sandals or barefeet in hot climates, your dog may want to have the same choice. The Neo Paws™ company does offer a summer shoe that has mesh uppers.

Rain Coats

Having foul weather gear to protect us from inclement weather is typical on most sailing boats. It is not as important for protection on powerboats where we can stay inside. The same is true for our pets.

Max and Bailey wear panchos; it helps keep them and the boat dry.

PHOTOGRAPH BY JANET PARKS

I must be honest in saying that I have not found a cruiser who has rain gear for a cat. That doesn't mean that it doesn't exist or that it isn't used. We think that most cats have already figured out that staying out of the rain is intelligent behavior and therefore don't need it. I have seen some dogs with rain gear but most cruisers don't find it necessary.

If you are going to be in rainy weather for several days, and you take your dogs ashore for walks, you may want rain gear for a very selfish reason. Living with wet dogs inside your boat is messy and smelly. Providing them with coats will not keep them totally dry but it helps. Keeping towels handy to dry them off as soon as they are below is helpful, but then you are stuck with wet towels. Max and Bailey are wearing human rain gear in this picture. Remember that if you use rain gear to protect your pets, use the PFD's on top if the weather is rough.

First Aid for Pets

10 In the process of writing this book, we came very close to losing Boca. If his problem had gone undiagnosed and untreated, which might have been the case at sea, he wouldn't be snoozing on our bunk at this moment. His condition was neither rare nor hard to treat, but we didn't expect him to be sick. Having a clear understanding of the types of problems your dog or cat can develop is critical to being prepared to cope with those problems.

In this chapter, we will discuss species-specific problems, but it is very complicated to deal with breed specific problems. If you plan to take your pet away from a source of immediate medical care, it is your responsibility to discuss this with your veterinarian. Be sure your veterinarian understands that not only will help be more remote, if you are in a foreign country, it could be inadequate.

This is the time to take an honest look at your pet's health. If you are dependent upon veterinary assistance, stay close to home. First aid is temporary help until you can get to a professional. If you know in advance that your pet requires regular, frequent professional care, think about the risk cruising involves. Knowingly putting your pet in peril is unconscionable.

If you expect to be at sea for a period of days, ask your veterinarian in advance if you can use email in case of an emergency. Remember, you must assume responsibility for your pet, and know what is an emergency before expecting your veterinarian to offer this type of assistance.

Medicine

Most cruisers prepare for human first aid and treatment while aboard. It is interesting to discover that some of those same items you need for yourself will also be useful for your cat or dog. The important thing about human medicines is to understand that dosages will be very different. Of course, some medications are not suitable for use in pet treatment. Beware of aspirin. We thought it was never appropriate to give it in any form to a cat. Robert Evans, DVM, said that there were extraordinary circumstances when a child's aspirin, 81 mg, could be given to a cat once every three days to relieve pain. It is given to dogs only under specific conditions.

Dr. Evans provided a list of some of those medicines you might have aboard that are appropriate for your dog or cat. Please note the brand name is followed by the generic name. This offers you the opportunity to find these medications in countries where pharmacology is not in English. You must know the weight of your pet; don't guess.

SYMPTOM	MEDICATION	GENERIC	DOG	CAT	DOSAGE
Vomiting	Tagament	cimetidine	X	X	5 mgr/ one lb every 12 hours
	Pepcid	famotidine	X	X	.5 mgr/ one lb once/twice daily
	Zantac	ranitidine	X		.5 mgr/ one lb twice daily
				X	1 mgr/ one lb twice daily
Diarrhea/colitis	Imodium	laperamide	X	X	.1mgr/ one lb every 12 hours
	Flagyl*	metronidazole	X	X	15mgr/ one lb twice daily
Infection	Amoxicillin		X	X	10mgr/ one lb twice daily
	Clavimax		X	X	10mgr/ one lb twice daily
	Ogmentin		X	X	10mgr/ one lb twice daily
	Keflex		X	X	20mgr/ one lb twice daily
	Bactrim		X	X	10mgr/ one lb twice daily
	Flagyl (as above)				
Wounds	hydrogen peroxide		X	X	clean three times daily
Dermatitis	Cortaid Crème		X	X	apply three times daily
Eyes	saline solution		X	X	to flush eye
	Artificial Tear				
	Ointment		X	X	three times daily for inflammation
Itch/Allergic Reaction (hive)					
	Benadyrl		X	X	1mgr/ one lb 2-3 times daily

The treatment for typical problems at sea—vomiting and diarrhea— are simple and Evans recommends the following:

For diarrhea, give water only, no food, for 24 hours. Then start with boiled rice until stools return to normal. Then offer a fifty/fifty mix of kibble and rice for two or three days.

For vomiting, give nothing for six to eight hours, and then offer a small amount of water hourly for four to six hours. Offer boiled rice 12-18 hours after the vomiting has ceased.

If either of these conditions persist after medication and the foregoing treatment, the condition may not be related to being at sea. Check further for other symptoms and get assistance as quickly as possible.

Treating seasickness in cats and dogs is similar to human treatment. Dramamine, dimenhydrinate, is the standard medication. Use it in quantities of four milligrams per pound of weight, two to three times daily. There is an important caution here. Do not give this medicine to hyperthyroid cats or to any pet with a cardiovascular condition or with epilepsy.

Medical Locker

Some cruisers organize their medical locker by types of problems. The items to treat burns are in one bag; orthopedic gear is in another bag, minor trauma in another bag, etc. For me that has not been a practical system. Zippers on bags freeze after being at sea for a time. Individual drawstring bags require dumping to find the needed items. The scissors are in the wrong bag. Worst of all, the bags mildew over time.

I prefer plastic boxes or baskets stacked in the locker so that I can see the contents and labels. All types of bandages are together. Medical equipment including a mercury bulb thermometer, tweezers, scissors, etc. is together. Note, you may have to search for a mercury bulb thermometer as they are less common. Ointments, creams, and salves that come in tubes are together. Pills are together, but divided into prescription and non-prescription. Bottles of over-the-counter liquids are together. How you organize these items needs to be efficient, clean, and easy for you.

You can make a separate bag or box for your pet or keep everything together. Some people might object to sharing a thermometer, so be sure that you have more than one aboard. If you need to measure amounts or cut pills to make the correct quantity for your small dog or cat, put a pill cutter and some measuring spoons in your medical equipment box. In specialty supply houses you can find tiny bottles or plastic bags to put dosages in if you are medicating your pet daily.

Since size is an issue if you have a pet aboard, include small ice bags, water bottles, blue ice bags to use on your pet. Add a roll of duct tape to use over bandages and to restrain your pet. If you need to put tape directly on fur or skin, low tack painter's tape is kinder to your dog or cat. No one likes to have hair ripped off by adhesive bandages.

One item peculiar to pet first aid is the cone or e-collar used to prevent a cat or dog from reaching a wounded area. Your pet will lick a sore or injury on his body and he will scratch wounds and sores on his face and head. The cone is fastened around the neck. It extends away from the neck keeping the head separate from the body. When your pet is wearing this device, he looks like his head is stuck through a lampshade or megaphone. Typically, the closure is some type of lacing and is adjustable. The cones in these photos are typical. We store the cone under a bunk mattress to keep it flat and out of the way.

Other items you are likely to have in a medical locker that are

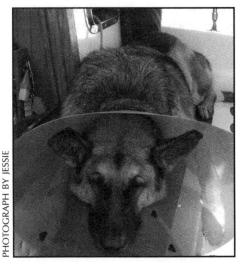

Cones are essential to recovery from a variety of ailments.

PHOTOGRAPH BY JESSIE

PHOTOGRAPH BY JESSIE

good pet first aid include antiseptic soap, an eyedropper, clippers or safety razor, tweezers or small needle nose pliers, ace bandages and triangle bandages.

Check the information in *Traveling with Your Pet* or in *The First Aid Companion for Cats & Dogs* for complete descriptions of pet first aid kits. You will find both books in the bibliography. The latter selection is a good reference to have on board. Be sure you review the medications, dosages, and equipment with your veterinarian.

Fleas

Boca was about five months old when we left home. His only exposure to the rest of the world was a required trip to the veterinarian to complete his shots and an overnight stay because he had hernia surgery. He did not have contact with other animals or with outdoor vegetation. He had neither fleas nor any other "bugs." Without getting off the boat, he contracted fleas.

Guests brought fleas aboard on their shoes and clothing. Fleas are common on the beach, in parks, and suddenly we had a problem. I read the labels on flea collars and they all indicated it wasn't safe to put the flea collar on a kitten. When we got to San Diego, I called a veterinarian. The doctor checked Boca and gave us a prescription for the fleas. We used Advantage™; it stopped the infestation, and ultimately ridded the boat and Boca of the fleas. At present, we find most veterinarians recommend using Advantage™ or Frontline™ for treating fleas. Flea powders or collars are designed to kill the adult flea. Unfortunately, they don't treat the animal so that future stages can't develop. The two flea preventatives are safe for cats and dogs. Your veterinarian can prescribe one of them for your pet. If you are at risk for future invasions of fleas, ask your veterinarian about taking a refill with you to use if needed.

Ear Mites and Fungus

Many cats and dogs develop ear mites. Kay on *Wave Dancer* said this about Schooner, "He had ear mites and fungus in his ears—possibly as a result of his 2-month stay with the veterinarian in air conditioning in Panama, during our home visit." Typically, your pet will communicate her ear problem by scratching. Occasionally your pet's balance is affected by ear problems. Poor balance or excessive scratching is a warning there may be a problem.

Mites are tiny parasites that are very hard to see. Generally, you will only find them in kittens and puppies. They are easily transferred among littermates. Pets that are under one year of age or have been living in crowded conditions with unowned pets are the most likely candidates for mites. If you notice a dark brown or black crumbly substance in your pet's ears, it may be an indicator of mites. The waste from the mites mixes with the wax from the ear to create the dirt. There are over-the-counter treatments or prescription medications available from your veterinarian. If your pet has a history of mites, be sure to include some type of medicine in the first aid kit.

The fungus that Kay referred to might also be a yeast infection. Moisture and lack of air circulation promote these types of infections. The infection is like athlete's foot of the ear. Treating with those medications you would use on your feet will work. Spritzing the ear with a mixture of equal parts of vinegar and water and then wiping the ear will help with this problem. The vinegar or the medications are acidic. They are effective because the infection results from a pH imbalance. The inflamed ear will be very sensitive and your pet may become agitated or angry about your treatment. Be careful!

Some pets have more difficulty if their ears are very furry and/or fold over so that air can't circulate. In this circumstance, it is a good idea to trim the fur carefully around the base of the ear to improve air circulation. After swimming, a bath, or an accidental dousing, make sure your pet's ears are dry. Use a small, flexible double-ended swab or cotton ball to reach the exposed part of the ear. As with human ears, sticking a long wooden swab or instrument into the ear could cause damage. Never use tissue or a washcloth; they are too harsh on the tender skin. Let only a trained veterinarian investigate the inner ear.

Heat Exposure

Your pet is susceptible to extremes in temperature just as you are. The normal temperature of a cat or dog is slightly higher than human averages; theirs is between 100.5 and 102 degrees while ours is 98.6. Unfortunately, this does not exempt your pet from suffering from too much heat. You need to exercise caution in warm weather.

The human body sweats as a mechanism for cooling. You know when your dog is warm because panting is its way of cooling. You may not realize that cats use grooming, which we equate with cleanliness, as a means of cooling. When a cat is panting, it is already over heated. If you are feeling uncomfortable in the heat, be aware that your pet is in the same boat.

First, be sure your pet has sufficient shade and water to keep cool. If the temperature exceeds your normal temperature, it is time for you and your pet to cool off. Provide cold water in whatever quantity your pet can consume.

Make a cold pack from towels and cold water to place on your pet. Place it in the groin area where the fur is thin. Isopropyl alcohol is also effective because it promotes rapid evaporation. If this isn't satisfactory, try putting your pet in a tub of water, a shower, or rinsing it with the anchor washdown. The latter is generally saltwater and you must rinse with fresh water to clean the salt from the fur. Many newer boats have outside shower areas that can be shaded and used for cooling.

Keep the air circulating. If the only shade is below decks, open hatches and ports. A small, 12-volt fan will increase evaporation for you and your pet and speed cooling. If your pet has long fur or matted hair, try brushing to fluff the coat and allow air into the skin. Pay attention to you pet's behavior. If it seems to have recovered, cease the application of ice and water, and remain in the shade.

Watch for unusual behavior in warm weather.

PHOTOGRAPH BY JESSIE

Poisoning

Your pet may run a greater risk of poisoning on board your boat than he does at home. Boats are self-contained so you carry cleaning products, antifreeze, pest-control products, and petroleum products on the boat. Add to that, those products are in accessible containers and locations for your convenience. Your pet will have easy access to dangerous materials unless you are alert to their dangers.

Cleaning products have acids and alkalis. It is hard to imagine that any animal would voluntarily ingest them, but it can happen. Because they attack the lining of the throat and stomach this is a situation where you don't want to induce vomiting; it will send those caustic chemicals back through the same tissue. Salad oil and bread will absorb those materials, and help relieve the pain. If the item was caustic, be sure to check for burns in the mouth and on the face. Sprits the burned area with cool water. Give them milk or water to relieve the pain until you can get to a veterinarian.

Antifreeze has a sweet flavor and is very tempting. Recently, some states have passed legislation to add a bitter flavoring to make it less palatable. If your pet has swallowed the antifreeze, you need to induce vomiting. Activated charcoal works and is available without prescription. Humans take it in tablet form but you will be better off with a liquid form. It isn't easy to administer but if you are faced with the situation where a veterinarian isn't available, use the charcoal.

Many marina areas have rats and vector control uses highly toxic bait to get rid of them. If your pet eats one of these compounds, she may become very sick. Internal bleeding often accompanies this kind of poisoning as well as seizures. It is important to induce vomiting. Your veterinarian or local poison control center can give assistance.

Petroleum products are everywhere on a boat. Kerosene for lanterns, gas for outboards, diesel for fuel, paint and more are too available. As with cleaning products, you don't want your pet to vomit. Give it bread and oil to absorb the poisonous material. If your pet vomits these materials, it could be absorbed into the lungs.

Both Dawn and Joy are detergents effective in cleaning petroleum products. If you can wipe the outsides of the containers when you put them away, you may avert a problem. If your pet gets the product on his coat, using a solution of one of these detergents for cleaning will help keep him from ingesting more. Use Vaseline to protect your pet's eyes from damage from petroleum products.

Cats can poison themselves in the process of grooming. If they get toxic materials on their fur, they may accidentally ingest it. Pay close attention when your cat comes back from a tour of the bilge or lockers. If the fur appears damp or shiny, check it carefully. Use a solution of the above referenced detergents followed with a quick rub down with a damp towel and then with another to dry if you suspect your cat has gotten into something you don't want him to lick off.

Again, if you plan to go offshore. Ask your veterinarian for specific instructions on administering antidotes and advice on how to feed your pet after this type of trauma.

Heimlich Maneuver

The pet food commercials showing dogs "wolfing" bowls of food always remind me of our family dog. No matter how recently he had eaten, the appearance of food set off an alarm in his mind that said, "This is the last food you will ever see." Inevitably, he gulped every last morsel. More than once the next few moments were filled with choking and coughing. He always recovered.

The eagerness and enthusiasm of pets when they eat is rewarding. Sometimes though, it can be scary if your pet begins to choke. Treat this situation in much the same manner you would treat each other using the Heimlich maneuver.

Before you attempt to administer the Heimlich, check the mouth and throat to see if the obstruction is visible and easily removed with your fingers. This may require two people, one to hold the animal's mouth open and the other to clear the mouth. Cats and dogs have very powerful jaws. They will react to your attempt to open the jaws and can accidentally inflict a major bite.

The Heimlich maneuver is used if your pet has choked and stopped breathing. For a cat or small dog you can hold them against your stomach and place your fist just below the rib cage. With your other hand over the fist make a quick inward and upward thrust. Try two or three times and then check to see if the object has come loose. However, remember, do this firmly, but gently. Small animals have small bones. Be careful not to break any. If you have a big dog, you will have to have her laying on her side on a rigid surface. With your knees against her back, place your fist just below the rib cage and thrust inward and upward sharply. You are attempting with the thrust to suddenly compress and force air upward out of the lungs through the throat.

Whether you are aiding a cat or dog, try to keep the head, throat, and back in line so that the opening is a straight line. This will facilitate your pet expelling the foreign object.

Artificial Respiration

If your pet stops breathing as a result of choking, once you have dislodged the object, you will need to administer artificial respiration. Close your pet's mouth and grasp it and the muzzle in one hand. Place your other hand on her chest to monitor breathing. Put your mouth over the nose and blow two puffs into her nose. You should feel the chest move with the incoming air. Continue with puffs into her nose at a rate of about 15 to 20 breaths per minute. Just as in humans, the lung size varies so puff gently with small dogs and cats. Blow only enough to elevate the chest of your pet. Big dogs will require stronger puffs, but remember blowing too hard will damage the lungs. If your pet does not start to breathe on her own, check again to make sure that the foreign object has been expelled.

Cardiopulmonary Resuscitation

CPR is taught in schools, businesses, and organizations for the protection of everyone. This same technique is used to protect your pet. This technique is designed to start the heart. As with humans, there are two components. One is breathing as described above in artificial respiration. The other component is heart compressions. Alternate these two components at a rate of one breath to five compressions.

If one person does compressions and a second does the breathing, the whole process is easier to maintain. Puppies and kittens require more than one compression per second which is very hard to do. Larger animals don't require as frequent compressions.

Important to any of the processes is knowing the anatomy of your animal so that you can check the vital signs. Your veterinarian can show you how to check pulse and heartbeat of your pet. Knowing where and how to apply pressure for any of these first aid techniques is critical to your success.

Euthanasia

Before going farther in this chapter, I need to warn you, the reader, that it may be difficult to deal with this topic. If you are not going offshore cruising with your pet, perhaps you would be happier skipping this section. The reason for including this section is best described through a letter received from my friend Mary, mentioned earlier in the book, who is cruising the Pacific with her husband, Terry, and until recently were accompanied by their two cats Rudder and Tiller.

"Rudder and Tiller are both (for me) heart breaking memories. While in Port Bonbonon on SE Negros, Rudder started getting sickly and losing weight. I took him to a veterinarian. The (sorry) moron said Rudder was constipated. He was almost afraid to touch him! I asked and asked that he take blood samples or tests of some kind but he wouldn't. It was a trip from hell getting him (Rudder) the 1 1/2 hours to and from Dumaguette on public transport. He slowly withered away even though Terry and I put him on antibiotics. We buried him on a hillside facing the western opening to the sunset. Tiller made it through most of Papua New Guinea but while in one of the atolls, he started having bladder problems again. I put him on antibiotics and thought it cleared up but the last atoll we were in, it got very bad. When we sailed out, we were in very big seas and every few seconds as we fell off a wave, Tiller would cry in pain. It makes me tear up just thinking about it. He didn't survive the passage to the Solomons and we buried him at sea.

"We tried to get our hands on a 'euthanasia kit' after Tiller died. To be completely honest, Tiller was suffering so badly (couldn't stand, labored breathing, lost bowel control) that we couldn't watch it anymore and Terry had to put him down himself. It would have been so much easier to have given him an injection. It would have prevented his (I'm humanizing here) feeling of betrayal, reduced his last moments of suffering and would have prevented our nightmares. No pet owner wants to think about this but it is a reality. It may be hard to find a veterinarian to give you what is required, but we met some South African expatriates who had a kit for their 16 year old dog so it is possible."

Sharing this letter in pet seminars, the audience sheds those tears for Mary and her cats. I have trouble holding them back each time I read the letter. Her final line in this letter prompted me to start asking questions.

Indeed, Robert Evans told me that it would be illegal for a veterinarian to put the drugs into the hands of an unlicensed person. He fully understands the problem, as he too is an ocean sailor. Finding a way to put a terminally ill animal out of misery is not easy. If you know in advance that this is a risk you face, then you must be prepared to cope with it. Not expecting your pet to die at sea from something that might be curable on land is an even harder situation with which you may have to cope.

There have been suggestions offered from a variety of people about how they would deal with this situation. One of the most reasonable sounding suggestions was to use tranquilizers such as Valium in a sufficient dosage that the sick animal would die quietly. Valium is a prescription drug that many cruisers have on board in case of panic.

The question raised at this suggestion is "What about big dogs?" Certainly, the 100-pound dog would require a huge dose for it to be fatal. It was suggested that a tranquilizer could be administered to calm a large dog and then suffocation with carbon dioxide from a fire extinguisher in a plastic bag would quickly finish the task of ending his life. I heard another individual say that they would use a gun to put a pet out of his misery. We have always discouraged firearms on a boat so that I don't consider it an option.

I don't know if I could do any of the things suggested. On the other hand, I am not sure what I would do if faced with the horrendous circumstances of watching a cherished friend die. At this point in time, unless you are licensed to carry the needed drugs for euthanizing a pet, there is no easy or ready answer. However, the risk remains and a prudent cruiser will have thought through this situation.

Safety for Pets

11 We address safety aboard our boats for our family, guests, and crew at every level of boating. Businesses, brokers, clubs, organizations, and government are all involved in promoting safe boating. Other than programs run through Boat US, we have not encountered programs designed to address safe boating with pets. We can practice some specific techniques with pets. These techniques should be known and practiced with all crewmembers physically able to participate.

Tania Aebi described for me the times when Tarzoon fell off the boat while underway. "He fell overboard twice, both times in the middle of the Indian Ocean. The first time, I saw it happen. We were heeled over, beating, and he slipped off the sprayhood and I was able to turn the boat around in time to save him. The second time, I never knew a thing until the unbecomingly wet kitty woke me up in the middle of a flat calm night, shaking water all over me and clamoring for a snack."

Pet Overboard Drill

All of us are quick to acknowledge the need for overboard drills. Unfortunately, fewer of us are eager to practice these drills. We toss life rings or life jackets in the water and bring the boat back to recover the objects. Unless the water is warm and the weather perfect, we rarely expect someone to voluntarily jump into the water and wait to be rescued.

If this is how we treat our family and crew, chances are very good, that we will operate the same way with the family pet. Sadly, the results are likely to be the same whether we are talking about practicing with people or pets. We will not be prepared.

Tania and Tarzoon's partnership survived two unplanned swims

First, being on deck underway should also mean wearing a personal flotation device (PFD). For humans, we can throw a horseshoe ring or deploy a Lifesling if someone has fallen overboard without a PFD. Cats and dogs aren't likely to use these devices. They don't have opposable thumbs for holding on tight. Even if they could grasp them in some manner, wakes, waves, and wavelets would make their grip tenuous. We know that children will be too frightened to respond so we require them to be jacketed on deck. The same rule should apply to your pet on deck.

If your pet falls overboard in calm conditions, she will be able to swim for a short time. You can go in after your pet. Even if you are a strong swimmer, do not get into the water without donning a PFD particularly if you are rescuing a two or four-footed crewmate. If you are cruising, you may have a dinghy on davits or on a tow. Getting into this smaller boat will make retrieving your pet easier as the freeboard is a matter of inches rather than feet. In either a large boat or dinghy, the wake you make under power heading toward a small animal in the water pushes the animal away. A large net on a handle, the type you would use to land a fish, is ideal for picking up a small pet. A larger pet might get a paw or two on such a net and be pulled in.

You are more likely to affect a rescue if your pet has a PFD or harness on. You can take a boat hook and put it through the handle on a PFD or the ring or strap of a harness. This will allow you to pull the animal alongside so he can be retrieved. Recently, we saw a large sailboat under power with crew and dog in the cockpit. The boat was under power in a canal and moving slowly when the dog went into the water. Two crewmembers jumped into the water after the dog. They were both wearing PFD's. Unfortunately, the dog was not wearing a PFD. He was a large Golden Retriever. The crew tried to lift the dog but the weight of the dog and the high freeboard of the boat made it impossible to get the dog aboard. Another, smaller boat, finally assisted them by picking up the dog. The only fortunate part of this incident was the arrival of the smaller boat to rescue the dog.

This was not an ideal pet overboard drill and it is not recommended. We do recommend that your pet practice being in the water with its PFD strapped on. Whether you do this from a dock, in a swimming pool, or from your boat, it is important for you to know exactly what is involved in getting your dog back on board. The things you don't want to discover in a real emergency are a badly fitted PFD, a dog that you can't lift from the water, or freeboard that is too high for you to retrieve your dog.

We have learned, from sad experience, that retrieving a cat is often dependent upon the cat. We now train our cat with a drill that may not be to his liking but works to save him. Many cruisers recommend leaving a heavy line with a knot, an old piece of carpet, or a bath towel hanging over the transom so your cat can climb aboard if he falls into the water. This is an excellent recommendation but falls short.

Your cat needs to learn how to use whatever item you trail off the transom. Our system is simple. Once our cat is big enough to get on deck by himself, he is big enough to learn about recovery. With my husband holding the painter of our dinghy, I sit on the bow of the dinghy holding the cat. With the dinghy against the transom of the boat, I put the cat's paws on the towel and slowly release my grip. Instinctively the cat's claws grab the towel. Without coaxing, he climbs the towel to the deck. After repeating this maneuver, my husband eases the painter so that the dinghy is not hard against the transom. This time without putting the cat's paws on the towel, I release the cat over the towel. He quickly responds by grabbing the towel and climbing on deck. The final step is to ease the painter so that there is water between the dinghy and the transom. I then release the cat in the water and he quickly grabs the towel and climbs the transom.

PHOTOGRAPH BY JESSIE

Training isn't fun, but the alternative is worse.

When another cruiser saw me train our cat, she was indignant at the idea of putting the cat in the water. I explained that we lost one cat because we didn't trail something overboard, and nearly lost a second cat because he couldn't find the towel. In a harsh voice I responded, "It is easier for me to rinse and dry a wet, angry cat than face pulling a drowned cat from the water." We do believe the drill works, and we do it in warm water. When Boca decided to swim in Puget Sound last year, he managed a quick rescue of himself from the cold water.

Whether you are training a cat or a dog, make sure that your wet pet is quickly clean and dried. When you are in salt water, be sure to rinse your pet with fresh water. Cats in particular are fussy about grooming and will attempt to lick all the salt from their fur at the first opportunity. If your cat goes in the water when you are in a harbor, there are likely to be less than healthy chemicals in the water that you don't want your cat to lick. We rinse them with slightly warm fresh water from the teakettle and then towel dry. If the water has been particularly cold, we hold the cat rubbing the fur with more dry towels. We have even used a 12-volt hair dryer on a low setting to warm the air in a box where we placed a cold, wet kitten.

Getting Back on Board

We have already described some of the problems getting on board from the water. Perhaps the two biggest issues with a pet are the size of the animal and the amount of freeboard your boat has. Once you have the pet and the boat, it is difficult to change the freeboard or the size of your pet. You will need other solutions.

Before anything else, the pet you are trying to rescue and anyone involved in the rescue needs to wear a PFD. The additional flotation will make the rescue easier. If you have a large dog, you may need assistance getting a PFD on the dog once it is in the water. It will instinctively want to paddle to stay afloat. Be familiar with how the PFD slips on and have the straps preset so you can work quickly. Take your dog and her PFD to the beach. Get into the water with your dog and actually put the wet PFD on the wet dog while you are standing on the solid bottom. This practice will give you and your dog practice and confidence in the procedure.

If you are working with a large dog, even if he is wearing a harness, you are wise to get a PFD on and use it for lifting. Normally a dog will not slip out of a harness, but suspending a big dog by his harness will be painful and could injure your dog.

If you have a swim platform, place your dog's front paws on the platform and try to boost your dog's hindquarters. If he is unwilling, use your shoulders as a platform for the dog to push from so he can get his hindquarters on the platform. Likewise, if you have a low transom where you can place the dog's front feet over the edge, boosting or aiding from the water will let him climb up. If the incline is too steep or your dog is too big, have someone wrap a large beach towel under the haunches and pull as you push the dog upward. Large dogs develop hip problems in their old age. Keep this in mind when pushing the dog onto a platform. A dislocated hip is far better than drowning, but an animal in pain is much less cooperative.

If there is no platform and the freeboard is too high, you will need to create lifting gear. Running lines or halyards under your dog's body could be harmful. If you have a sling arrangement for your dinghy or outboard, it may work on your dog. Better yet, plan ahead, and make a sling of webbing that is at least three inches wide. Just as you see with most vests, there should be at least two straps under the body so that the weight is evenly distributed. A sling of canvas with straps on the four corners might be easier to get a large dog into. Those straps can be brought together in pairs, which distributes weight evenly and is more manageable. Use the largest winch you have aboard and take

PHOTOGRAPH BY RUFFWEAR

Practice with PFD's in shallow water.

the dog slowly out of the water and on to the deck. Prevent the halyard swinging by attaching a line to it, to restrain it.

Larger powerboats and sailboats have dinghies on davits or hoists. Lowering the dinghy and pushing your big dog into it is the quickest retrieval system. Once your dog is in the dinghy you can raise the dinghy on its hoist or davits and bring your dog aboard. Be sure you get your dog clean and dry as soon as possible. Even big dogs can become hypothermic.

Lifejackets

We have already spent a great deal of time on the types of flotation devices available for your pet. Having a PFD for your pet is essential. It must be one that fits snugly without preventing leg motion. The straps must be adjustable and easy to fasten. Ideally the device will be yellow or orange, and have reflective stripes as well. A handle that will sustain your pet's weight while it is being lifted is clearly an advantage. The most important factor is wearing it.

Having said it must be worn, we take exception to that in some degree with cats. Some cats will freeze when you put a PFD on them. Many cats have difficulty in walking and climbing while wearing a PFD. Much of the cat's ability to move and climb is restricted by a bulky PFD. We tried a number of different PFD's but found most of the small sizes did not fit our 15-pound cat without additional adjustments. It is easy enough to take up the extra slack in the straps and cut off the excess. Those straps that are designed to fit without adjustment devices need to be trimmed and re-stitched or have tucks put into the straps.

Many cat owners have a different "take" on using a PFD. Kay Malseed said of Schooner, "He wears no harness or leash and we are opposed to a life jacket which would prolong suffering if he were lost overboard, not recovered."

Jenni said of Polar the Wonder Cat, "He's worn a safety harness—complete with bungee chord—and refused to wear a PFD, which ended up being given to a friend's dachshund of about the same weight, who didn't have Polar's sense of haut couture."

We haven't used a PFD on any of our cats while cruising. We haven't found anything that doesn't encumber a cat's natural agility. It needs to be able to jump and climb. Boca's reaction to heavy weather is to get as far as possible from whatever he perceives as disagreeable. He can be managed with a harness and he can rescue himself from non-moving situations. We will continue to search to find something appropriate to a cat.

Cats don't stay on deck during rough weather if given a choice. They find a place to burrow until the nasty stuff blows over. The risk factor for cats is less than for dogs; the latter generally prefer to be close to owners when the going gets rough.

There are no standards for buoyancy, weight, or durability for pet PFD's. Remember that USCG approved floatation is designed to keep you floating in an upright position with your hands and legs free to move and cooperate with rescuers. The pet PFD by contrast is basically a lifting device and swimming aid. It is not guaranteed and thorough testing by you is your only warranty the PFD will work as you want it to.

Harness and Lifelines

If you are concerned about keeping your dog on deck, especially underway, you may want to approach this situation the same way you would for the rest of your crew. String static lines from the bow to the stern on both sides of the boat. They are made of nylon webbing of a high test so they can sustain the weight of your heaviest crew. They are flat, laid on deck, permitting crew to snap on a lifeline at any point. The lifeline tether is short. The idea behind this arrangement is protection if you slip accidentally or are struck by a wave. The short tether will keep you on board. If you wore a long tether, you could very well end up in the water being dragged by the boat, if you slipped. The same principle is true for your dog underway. A short tether will allow your dog to walk on deck without worrying about being swept overboard.

Don and Ellen Freeman concocted a special harness for Tristan. They sewed two regular harnesses together so that two straps encircled the rib cage and one strap ran across the chest. With the D ring on the lateral strap, Tristan can be lifted quickly without pain.

Clearly, hooking on to a static line is to allow safe movement about

PHOTOGRAPH BY DON FREEMAN

The homemade three part harness is an excellent idea.

the deck. In the cockpit, there should be places into which you can snap a tether. We have places at the steering station and a couple near the companionway. At the steering station, we replace one of the pedestal bolts with an eyebolt. If your dog is more comfortable being near you in the cockpit, there should be a sturdy ring for his tether hook. Again, the length of the tether should be half the width of the cockpit. This will allow your dog to be in the cockpit, not underfoot, but not likely to be thrown overboard.

It is understood that this type of tether is always fastened to a harness rather than a collar. The sudden motion on a sailboat as it falls off a wave could easily break a dog's neck. Use a strong harness, nylon webbing as we described earlier, and stainless or bronze D rings.

If you leave your pet alone on your boat, it is safest to put her below. If you think the temperature of the boat is a problem, create more air circulation or additional screening to keep your pet cool while keeping her below. Leaving your pet alone on deck is asking for disaster. We think that our pet onboard, alone at anchor is relatively safe. Unfortunately, we know from experience that this isn't true. Some cruisers have left pets on board, alone, and on a tether. If your pet gets excited in these conditions, she may attempt to jump overboard. If she has a harness on, she could spend hours suspended and possibly get hurt. If she has a tether on a collar and goes overboard, you will probably return to a strangled pet. Remember, when you are away from the boat, your pet is very likely to want company and may try to join a passing boat, kayakers, or swimmers.

Abandon Ship

The time to abandon ship is when you have to climb up into the life raft. That may sound like an overstatement, but it is true that many lives have been lost because the decision to abandon ship for the life raft was made unnecessarily. If you think about the difference between being on a boat and in a life raft, it is obvious that even a boat that is damaged has a better chance of being found than a small raft. After some of the most severe storms at sea, damaged hulls are still afloat while the crew has gone in a life raft and is never recovered.

Taking a pet into a life raft is not an experience I have had. It is not an experience that I want. Several cruisers have said to me that their pet would be the first in the life raft because of their importance in the owner's life. From the point of practicality, it doesn't seem like the most logical sequence. If you are attempting to get a pet into a raft in an emergency, he will be terrified. It may be possible to stuff him quickly into a carrier and pass him to the raft. A cat or small dog can be handed from one person to another. This is the time that everyone including pets must be in PFD's. A big dog must get into the raft with a minimum effort from you and the person in the raft. This may be the point at which you have the most difficulty if your pet has not been fully trained to get in and out of the dinghy on command.

In August of 2002, the USCG rescued a man and his son, and the family dog from the cold waters of the North Pacific. Jim Bingman, his 13-year-old son, and their two-year old yellow Labrador were underway from Bristol to Ketchikan, Alaska. In that part of the world, people travel by air or water. They were moving their fishing boat to Ketchikan. They struck some debris in the water and lost power. The fishing boat was taking on water. Jim was trying to bail with one bucket; the second bucket had already been lost. To keep Justin busy, they inflated the life raft. Jim had Justin organize the dinghy and hang on to the painter to keep the raft close by.

Their two-year old dog, Honey, is not fond of water. Jim put her in her PFD, taped her paws so that her nails wouldn't cut the dinghy, and loaded her in the dinghy with Justin. After nearly two hours of bailing, Justin couldn't hold the painter anymore and the raft drifted away from the damaged boat. Jim jumped in and swam to the raft. They set off their 406 EPIRB and waited. The rescue team arrived in a helicopter and one of the swimmers jumped in to help get the three from the raft into the basket of the helicopter. Justin and Jim were rescued first; then the swimmer went back for Honey.

She was very frightened and docile. Jim describes her as having a sweet disposition and they have never seen a display of temper. The swimmer grabbed the handle of her PFD and pulled Honey in the water. He swam on his back with Honey's paws over his arm. Honey rode the basket up to the helicopter and her waiting family. Reportedly, she wasn't afraid of the flight although it was quite noisy.

Unbeknownst to her rescuer, Honey was a very pregnant pooch. According to Jim, one month later she gave birth to nine live puppies. The story has a happy conclusion because of preparation. The PFD

PHOTOGRAPH BY JIM BINGMAN

A PFD, liferaft, EPIRB, and USCG made it possible for Honey to be the mother of nine.

worked for Honey. Taping her paws assured safety in the raft. Carrying an up-to-date EPIRB insured that they were quickly located.

There are stories of rescue from huge commercial vessels as well as small boats where dogs have resisted rescue because they were terrified. A large Indonesian tanker was sinking on March 13, 2002. It was a serious situation; one man had already been killed by fire. The situation was serious because the ship had neither power nor communication. On April 2, a nearby cruise ship rescued the crew of 11 taking them to safety. Unfortunately, the captain's dog was not rescued. Stories vary as to whether the captain didn't want to impose on the rescuers or if they did not want to take the dog on board or if she just panicked. Hokget, which translates as good fortune, remained aboard this drifting hulk.

The Humane Society of Hawaii and the Humane Society of the United States stepped in on behalf of the stranded pooch and hired the American Marine Corporation to rescue the dog. Keeping track of a ship in the North Pacific is not a simple matter when there is no signal aboard. After a futile search, in more than 14,000 square miles of water the Hawaiian Humane Society called off the search. The

American Marine Corp. took over and continued coordinating the search on their own time. The search continued and follow-ups were made on reported sightings, but the weather turned bad and everyone feared the worst. Finally, the ship was spotted not far from Johnston Island by a USCG C-130 returning to Hawaii.

On April 20, they verified the location of the ship. One

Hokget became famous for surviving 24 days on a sinking ship.

of the crew thought there was a dog onboard. They had been filming the tanker with a video camera and rewound the tape to verify what the crew member reported. Indeed, there was a dog seen running across the deck. The crew was relieved and amazed to see that the dog was still alive after three solitary weeks. The crew of the plane collected all of the food they had aboard and put it into a sonar buoy case. They were low on fuel but made one more pass over the deck, dropping the box of food. The box broke open on impact spewing cookies, cake, fruit, energy bars, and pizza all over the deck. Granted it was not a typical dog diet, but acceptable under the circumstances.

The fishing community responded to a USCG bulletin asking for assistance in rescuing Hokget. *Pacific Fin* and the *Marie M*, located the hulk and sent crew aboard to find the dog. After searching for two days they failed to find Hokget but left food for the dog. They returned to fishing and reported the situation to the USCG.

The drift rate of the abandoned tanker represented a threat to the wildlife sanctuary on Johnston Atoll. The USCG sent in *American Quest*, the tugboat from American Marine Corp, to bring the ship to Hawaii. Before the tug arrived a C130 flew over the tanker tracking its drift and found no sign of the dog. The *American Quest* reached the tanker on April 26 and the crew found the frightened dog cowering in the forward section.

The story has a happy if prolonged ending. Hokget had to spend the mandatory 120-day quarantine in Hawaii before she could be released. The ship captain asked that a friend in Hawaii take custody of his dog. On August 30, a very celebrated survivor was the feature of a major news conference in Honolulu. She established a record that no one hopes to break—24 days alone on a sinking boat.

Boating safety is and has always been the responsibility of the captain. If you are going to take your pet aboard, then you are responsible for him as well. Plan ahead for your pet just as you would for your crew. If you can't make it as safe for your pet to be aboard as for your crew, then leave your pet at home.

Foreign Travel

12 Cruising is a form of travel, and staying in your home waters and your home state avoids complications that are automatically a part of foreign travel. Whether you are cruising at home or abroad take your pet in for a check up; have his shots updated. Your veterinarian is best equipped to diagnose a problem that is latent and could erupt on your trip. If you have determined that your pet is prone to seasickness, ask the veterinarian to prescribe an appropriate drug for him.

Health Certificates

A basic requirement for traveling cats or dogs is a health certificate. Your veterinarian can provide you with this document. It will show proof that your pet is healthy, has up-to-date immunizations, and is not carrying potential problems for you or the venue you plan to visit. Traveling in the United States is simple as long as you have proof of current rabies vaccination. There is one major exception in US travel. Hawaii has strict requirements that include a period of quarantine. We will examine these requirements more completely later in the chapter.

Most veterinarians can provide an International Health Certificate for your pet. If you are leaving for a foreign port, the majority of countries will require that your certification has been completed within 30 days of your departure. Some countries, notably Mexico, want the certification to be within two weeks of the day of entry. We have encountered some information that says the certification must be within 72 hours of entering Mexico. The international certificate will provide more detailed immunization information. Most countries will require vaccinations for rabies. Other immunizations include distemper, hepatitis, and Lyme disease among others. They may also require tests proving your pet does not have heartworms. This certificate will also be specific in describing your animal.

An international health certificate may require validation. Again, as an example, Mexico requires that the United States Department of Agriculture (USDA) verify your pet's certificate. The validation process requires sending the veterinarian's completed certificate along with the necessary fee to your nearest USDA office. The purpose is to give governmental sanction to your certificate. If you're unsure about your travel plans, sending in your pet's certificate for validation would be a smart plan. We treat that international certificate with the same care as we do our personal passports.

Rabies Is Your Problem

Rabies is a disease known throughout the world. As a pet owner and a cruiser, you must follow the regulations in your own country and the ones you visit. In the United States, Canada, Mexico, and most of the countries you would visit by boat, rabies vaccinations are required for cats and dogs. Some countries are more vigorous in enforcing the rules, but the requirements exist nonetheless. Some countries are rabies free. They have tough regulations in place to maintain that rabies free status.

One of the most shameful moments I remember as a cruiser, is listening to another American complain about the tough rules regarding rabies. This person went on at great length about how unfair it was to put an immunized animal in quarantine. My response to that complaint was that if you plan to visit a country with strict rules, plan to live with the rules. Others have tried to subvert the rules through a rendezvous with a local boat to transfer the incoming pet, or use the document from another pet of similar description that has completed quarantine. This behavior puts the rest of us cruising with our pets in a tough situation. We are all painted with the same brush.

Anyone who thinks that his or her cat or dog is more important than the health or economy of an entire country should not cruise. They will disrupt a lifestyle that many of us cherish. They are better off staying at home and traveling by car or plane. The penalties for breaking regulations include fines and euthanizing the pet. The pet owner will live to own another pet. I hope that my personal position is clear on this issue.

Microchips

Tags and tattoos are no longer the standard for identification of a pet. The new technology for identification in the pet owning community is the microchip. This tiny chip, about the size of a grain of rice, is implanted under the skin of a cat or dog. Using a hypodermic needle, the microchip is inserted under the loose skin between the shoulder blades. This is a painless process requiring no anesthesia. It is a permanent implant providing identification of your pet for life. The implanted microchip is read with an electronic reader or scanner. The scanner picks up the unique code from the chip. This code is then matched through a central identification bank with your name and telephone number. In the United States, we have at least two types of chips and data banks available that include your pet in this identification program.

The American Veterinary Identification Device (AVID) is a chip marketed and used through the veterinary association. It maintains a databank called PETtrac. The Home Again Identification Program uses the Friend Chip from the Schering Plough Company. Although the two chips have different manufacturers, there are universal scanners or readers now available. Equipment to read either one of these chips is in veterinary centers, pet shelters, emergency hospitals, and local animal control centers. Scanners that are not universal readers do indicate what type of chip is implanted even when it cannot decipher the specific code. We have listed several websites with information about obtaining the microchip in the appendix.

Many countries have the microchip program in place and have requirements about local and alien pets being identifiable by scanning. In Europe, companion dog microchips are required for all dogs. In Canada and Great Britain the programs are in place and widely used. The location and return rate of lost pets in those countries using the chips is substantial. The rate of return in the United States has improved because owners are "chipping" their pets. Owners of pure-bred pets were the first to use this program nationally, but it is becoming more common throughout the country.

The implantation of a microchip is not required in the US but it is recommended if you plan to cruise to foreign ports and Hawaii. A pet with a microchip and meeting local health requirements often is exempted from lengthy quarantines. In some countries, the penalty for failure to "chip" your pet is quite harsh. In Hong Kong, euthanizing is automatic for a dog without a chip. Friends in Hong Kong had their cats chipped because soon cats will come under a similar rule. In Hawaii, one of the requirements for a shortened quarantine is a microchip. To be considered for a shortened quarantine period in Australia, the microchip is required. In the United Kingdom, some foreign pets that have the microchips are exempted from quarantine.

Whether or not you plan extended cruising, the implantation of a microchip may save you and your pet from the agony of separation. Your local veterinarian typically can arrange the implant. A quick telephone survey revealed prices from $30 to $90 for implantation. Some of these fees included giving the pet a physical if she did not already have a history with the veterinary hospital. Most microchip systems offer a tag with the registration number that is on the chip. That tag can be attached to a collar or harness. The only caveat within the identification process is that you must keep your contact information up-to-date.

There are programs offered in some states through pet shelters where there are clinic days for the sole purpose of implanting microchips at a minimal cost. The humane society supports regular programs that combine spaying/neutering, vaccinations, and microchip implant. You may find it worth your while to look for one of these clinics and get a package deal.

There is some misinformation about these microchips leftover from the early introductory period. The cost is not exorbitant. We paid $58 for implanting the chip and $12.50 for registration with the data bank. The microchips last for the life of the animal and they do not migrate in the pet's body. The microchips have acquired limited legal status as identification. They serve as proof of ownership in the American Kennel Club. Moreover, it has been suggested that the microchip is the determining factor in the custody of a pet.

Quarantine Procedures

If you travel from country to country, you have to repeat the process of verification of the health and status of your pet. With varying deadlines, it will seem extremely difficult to take your pet from country to country. Actually, with some patience, you will find some advantages to preplanning.

First, you need to discover the rules for the first country that you plan to visit. A rule of thumb is that most island countries will have some form of quarantine. Please don't feel insulted if you think we are calling Australia an island. They have been formidable enforcers of their quarantine regulations and have managed to protect their entire country's agricultural economy.

On the East Coast of North America, you will find that many islands in the Atlantic and Caribbean have tough rules. If you plan to visit Antigua, Barbuda, Barbados, Caymans, Guadeloupe, Jamaica, Martinique, Montserrat, St. Kitts and Nevis, and St. Vincent and the Grenadines, contact the embassy or consulate for a copy of the regulations. Do this at least six months in advance as testing requirements and immunizations needed before issuance of a health certificate will be time consuming.

On *Wave Dancer,* Kay Malseed said their experiences with Schooner have been positive. "Schooner moved aboard when we bought the boat in June 1995 and has traveled through both eastern and western Caribbean, Trinidad, Venezuela, Aruba, Bonaire, Curacao, Jamaica, Grand Caymans, Mexico, Panama, Galapagos, and French Polynesia. Third world countries have demonstrated very little interest in him—seldom asking for his medical papers. We had a microchip implanted in Panama to assist with his eventual entry into New Zealand or Australia.

"Our first encounter with government regulations was when the veterinarian boarded our vessel in Papeete, verified that Schooner had NOT left the boat since we departed Panama in March and that he qualified for the six months "involuntary or self-imposed" quarantine enroute to Tahiti. She provided documentation of her examination and noted the fact she dusted him for fleas and administered a shot for internal parasites—at no charge! We considered flying home to visit Washington state but were informed WE could purchase round-trip tickets for ourselves, but Schooner would only be issued a ONE-WAY, as he couldn't re-enter since they have no quarantine facility! Schooner is quite content to remain on board, disinclined to "jump ship" even if the dock is less than a foot away."

Be aware that there is often a difference between what tourist offices and agricultural or animal quarantine offices will tell you about their country's regulations. We have found some major variations between the promulgated practices and what happens when you arrive. One cruiser reported that the following countries allowed landing of their dog without quarantine: Bahamas and British Virgin Islands. In other islands—Antigua, Montserrat, St. Kitts-Nevis, St. Lucia, and St. Vincent and the Grenadines—the animals were landed and then local veterinarians said that dogs were not permitted. This frustrating situation will become more complicated before it is simplified.

In Trinidad and Tobago, there is a directory published annually by Boaters' Enterprise Ltd. that includes quarantine information. Jack Dausend annually updates the regulations for visiting cruisers. He also has a website, which we have listed, that is even more current should there be changes in government regulations. Unfortunately, this type of up-to-date source is not available in most of the island countries.

The government of Great Britain has been the standard in many countries, especially those in the Caribbean, because they have had strict quarantine policies for more than a century. Recently, a program called the Pet Travel Scheme (PETS) was begun that allows pets from specific countries to be exempted from quarantine. The exemption is dependent upon the pet having a current rabies vaccination and proof thereof, a microchip for identification, and a blood test certified by a veterinarian. Papers must be filed before the pet's arrival but then the animal will be free to travel in Great Britain.

At present, the following countries are included in PETS: Antigua and Barbuda, Ascension Island, Australia, Barbados, Bermuda, Cayman Islands, Cyprus, Falkland Islands, Fiji, French Polynesia, Guadeloupe, Hawaii, Jamaica, Japan, La Reunion, Malta, Martinique, Mauritius, Mayotte, Montserrat, New Caledonia, New Zealand, St Helena, St Kitts and Nevis, St, Vincent, Singapore, Vanuatu, Wallis and Fortuna. All of these countries and territories are islands except the continent of Australia.

This program was extended to include the United States and Canada in November of 2002. In so doing, those countries in the Caribbean that have used Great Britain as the standard, will find themselves faced with major revision of their practices. Whether there will be a reciprocal agreement between the countries qualified for PETS is an open question. The text of the announcement is in the appendix.

Unfortunately, any companion pet that arrives in Great Britain via a private yacht is not covered under this program. The specific comment from the government follows:

> "One of the criteria for entry into the UK once all the procedures have been met is that the animal arrives into the UK by means of an approved carrier. The interpretation of an approved "carrier" means any undertaking carrying goods or passengers for hire by land, sea, or air.
>
> "Ultimately, participation in the Scheme is a commercial decision by the carriers, if they wish to participate a system of auditing and inspection of carriers and their facilities will be put into place. These checks will provide a safeguard to ensure that carriers comply fully with prescribed procedures.
>
> "Therefore entry into the UK with animals is not permitted by means of a private vessel."

The full context of the letter is in the appendix under the Quarantine Information for Great Britain. The very specific statement requiring arrival on a commercial carrier does seem difficult to circumvent. However, if you can organize meeting the requirements you might be able to arrange shipping your cat or dog and picking it up. Many cruisers fly home in the winter leaving their boats in the UK. It might be possible to have a crew or family member bring your pet via a commercial carrier. It is something to consider.

There is a concerted effort to speed the clearance process and do away with quarantine. Determining the health of animals that apply in advance is possible especially with the advent of chip identification, which is almost impossible to avoid.

I heard from Ann Hoffner about Pearl, her gray cat cruising on S/V

Oddly Enough regarding quarantine procedures in Tahiti. "We are presently in French Polynesia, and Pearl is in quarantine that started when she left the last port that was not rabies free. This should have been Panama, but the government veterinarian who came on board to see her in Papeete was a substitute and marked her down as rabies free since Galapagos. When her six months are up, we can get papers to that effect, but if we go to New Zealand or Australia, or Hawaii, she will still have to go under their quarantine rules. Before we leave Papeete we plan on getting her rabies vaccine updated, and having a microchip implanted."

Until a decision in favor of PETS reciprocity, the West Coast of North America, Hawaii, Fiji, French Polynesia, New Caledonia, New Zealand, Vanuatu, and Australia treat your dog or cat as if PETS did not exist. Study the specific regulations about pet quarantine well in advance.

Hawaii

The quarantine packet and rules from Hawaii are extensive. You will need plenty of time to meet all of the requirements. However, if you do meet the requirements, then you will have only a 30-day quarantine as opposed to 120 days of quarantine. There is a worksheet provided that will help the owner determine what must be done to qualify for the short-term quarantine. These are the basics of those requirements. All dogs and cats entering Hawaii are required to have a health certificate, an implanted electronic microchip, and meet the vaccinations' requirements. It is the owner's responsibility to have the microchip implanted by a veterinarian and ensure the microchip number is recorded on the serum sample submitted for the rabies testing. The microchip number must be included on the results of the rabies test.

These are the specific regulations provided by the State of Hawaii in order to qualify for 30-day quarantine.

1. A minimum of two (2) rabies vaccinations not less than 6 months apart with an approved monovalent inactivated rabies vaccine.
   a. The first vaccination shall not be given less than 3 months of age;
   b. The second or subsequent vaccination shall be given no less

than 90 days and not more than 12 months before arrival in Hawaii;

   c. The name, serial or lot number, expiration date of the lot and date and route of administration must appear on the health certificate; and

   d. Information for the two most recent rabies vaccinations shall be recorded on the health certificate.

2. OIE Fluorescent Antibody Virus Neutralization (OIE FAVN test) A rabies blood test (requiring 1 to 3 ml. Of serum) to determine if dogs and cats have responded adequately to rabies vaccination is required prior to arrival to qualify for the 30-day quarantine. The testing laboratory must submit the test results directly to the Animal Industry Division. 99-941 Halawa Valley Street, Aiea, Hawaii 96701.

   a. The OIE-FAVN test must be conducted no less than 90 days and not more than 12 months prior to arrival in Hawaii. A result of 0.5 I.U. per milliliter of rabies antibodies or greater is required. The day following the date the laboratory receives the OIE-FAVN sample is the beginning date for the 90-day countdown.

   b. To be considered valid, the test results must include the number of the implanted microchip and a completed description of the animal (age, sex, breed, color or color pattern, any visible unique identifying characteristics, etc.).

   c. A sample of whole blood cells must also be submitted to the testing laboratory. Have your veterinarian submit a 1 to 3 milliliter heparinized or EDTA blood collection tube. The laboratory shall hold the blood sample in until 120 days after arrival of the animal into Hawaii. The blood cells may be used at a later date for genetic analysis to confirm the identity of a dog or cat.

3. Health Certificate—A health certificate issued by an accredited veterinarian within 14 days prior to arrival is required. (Check with the specific airline regarding their health certificate time requirements.) The health certificate must be written in English, be an original document (not a facsimile or photocopy), bears an original or carbon signature and legible name, address and

telephone number of the certifying veterinarian. The health certificate must also contain the following information:

a. A complete description of your pet including age, markings, sex, breed and any additional identifying characteristics.

b. Written declaration by issuing veterinarian that the animal was treated to kill all ticks and other external parasites within 14 days prior to arrival except when a veterinarian provides a written statement that such treatment may be detrimental to the animal's health. List the name of the treatment used and the date of the treatment.

c. Certification that your pet is free of any evidence of infectious or contagious disease.

d. For dogs, date and results of heartworm test performed within 14 days prior to arrival.

e. Certification by the issuing veterinarian to the accuracy of the information stated on the health certificate.

f. Record of all required vaccinations. For rabies vaccinations, the name of the vaccine, lot/serial number, expiration date of the lot, and date and route of administration must be included. To qualify for 30-day quarantine, list information on the two (2) most recent rabies vaccinations.

g. The microchip number and date of implantation. You will find the contact information for Hawaii in the appendix.

We stopped in Honolulu enroute from Acapulco to Manila. The authorities knew that we were coming and that we had Boca aboard. When we tied up at the dock, the quarantine officers were on hand and brought a carrier aboard. They immediately put Boca into the carrier and then we filled out the papers. The officers knew that we would be in Honolulu for a week. We showed them the certificate of health, and the immunization records for those vaccinations since the issuance of the certificate. We knew that Hawaii required a certificate that was no more than 14-days old. We had a rugged trip and it took 23 days to get to Honolulu from Acapulco. Our original USDA certification was two years old and our endorsement from a Mexican veterinarian was six months old. We weren't interested in qualifying for a 30-day quarantine because we knew it was a short layover. The officers took Boca to "kitty kamp" with an appointment to return the following Saturday.

In Hawaii, the quarantine facilities are excellent. Each dog lives in a large kennel. The small dogs, toy varieties and others under 30 pounds have kennels that are about 12 feet in length, while bigger dogs get more space. The biggest dogs appeared to have a total length of 18-20 feet. All of the kennels were fenced with a solid roof and concrete flooring. The back section of each kennel was enclosed for privacy and most dogs had beds or crates in the back of their enclosure. The kennels are about five to six feet wide and about eight feet high. Owners may groom, feed, and walk their dogs. The kennel staff walks and feeds dogs where owners don't attend. I saw one situation where a dog had two flats of turf in his kennel. The owner walked and fed his dog because it bit strangers. The grass turf was in place in the event the owner didn't make it to the kennel on time.

The catteries were spread throughout the complex. Each cattery, a large lanai-type building, held about 40 cats in individual kennels. The cats had spaces about six feet by ten feet deep, and eight feet high. The back part of each space opened to the outside. A long aisle ran through the middle of the cattery so that the keepers could feed and care for the cats. Cat owners were also welcome to feed and visit their pets. The interior of each space held a litter box, a feeding area, a sleeping area, and a climbing area. The climbing area was a series of

Hawaii's quarantine for dogs is "plush."

PHOTOGRAPH BY JESSIE

ramps that went to the top of the space. The ramp ended with a platform. Whoever designed the kennel spaces understood the need for cats to climb and look down on their territory.

The entire setting was park-like with lawns, cement walkways, and palm trees. The staff was knowledgeable about their charges. They also showed a very positive attitude toward the cats and dogs. They knew how to comfort the lonely ones.

We had many repairs to do before moving on, and we were glad to have Boca in such good hands. We paid the registration fee of $35 plus $7.50 per day for his care. At the appointed time, the officers returned Boca to us and put him on the boat. The officers stayed on the dock until we actually cast off and cleared the harbor.

Reading all of the foregoing may sound onerous but there is an upside to this. Cruisers who have qualified in Hawaii by meeting the requirements and going through the 30-day quarantine, are exempted from quarantine in many other places in the Pacific. If you come to Hawaii directly from New Zealand, Australia, and the British Isles, you are likely to be exempted from Hawaiian quarantine. Because the rabies rules are stringent, it may be worth your while looking into qualifying your pet.

PHOTOGRAPH BY JESSIE

Cat quarters in the Honolulu Q. station have great climbing ramps.

PHOTOGRAPH BY JESSIE

The park-like quarantine station is a great temporary home.

There was an attempt in July of 2002 to remove the quarantine requirement in Hawaii. A large group of citizens brought the request to the Board of Directors of the State Agriculture Department. Unfortunately, they were severely rebuffed when the vote was seven to zero in favor of keeping the quarantine in place. There has been much publicity and the issue is certain to reappear again.

Guam

After Hawaii, our next stop was Guam. Guam has very tough quarantine regulations concerning rabies, similar to those in Hawaii. However, we anchored in the harbor nearly a mile from the shore facilities. When we checked into Guam, we said that we had a cat aboard. We were asked if we planned to bring the cat ashore. When we answered in the negative, the officers said that we would not be required to put the cat in quarantine. We assumed they thought Boca wouldn't willingly try to swim ashore. They were right. Staying on board constituted his quarantine.

However, our experience was with a cat. Dogs are likely to be treated differently and leaving your dog aboard at anchor is difficult. The Pet Quarantine Law of 1998 requires 120-day quarantine for pets. The port from which the pet arrives determines the location of the quarantine. Most pets that are from Pacific Rim countries or islands are permitted to stay in quarantine in Guam. All other pets are required to serve quarantine in Hawaii (it does sound like a jail sentence). For vessels from the United States, the pets on board may stay in quarantine in Guam except for those from Puerto Rico, and those from the border counties in Texas, New Mexico, Arizona and California. Mexico is not deemed rabies free so the border counties are treated as a similar risk.

Australia

Several years ago, cruising friends in Australia did not choose to qualify for importation via quarantine. They did not plan to remain in the country long enough to make the effort seem worthwhile. The alternative for them was difficult. The boat was not permitted alongside any piers, docks, or other facilities where a dog or cat could disembark. They had to anchor away from shore and keep their pet aboard. In addition, they were required to post a bond with the government quarantine office. An inspector visited the boat at the anchorage frequently to verify that the animal was aboard. They were told that the penalties for the animal leaving the boat included forfeiting the bond and the animal being euthanized. This situation occurred before the introduction of microchip rules.

Australia is a choice cruising destination. Rules have changed a great deal over the years, so I asked the Australian government to explain the current situation. This was the response from Noelene McLennan of the Quarantine and Inspection Service at the time of publication.

"Yachts visiting Australia with pets aboard must call at an AQIS-controlled port and identify themselves to the AQIS office. AQIS will issue a Master's Notice detailing conditions during the yacht's stay in Australia. The Master's Notice will be valid for a period of 3 months, and the conditions include restrictions such as deep-water anchorage only, regular inspections by an AQIS officer, provision of a strict itinerary for the yacht's movement within Australian waters, and confining animals below when owners not present aboard. All charges associated with issue of the Master's Notice and AQIS surveillance of the yacht must be met by the animal's owner. Alternatively, you may choose to arrange for import of your dog/cat, which will then mean that the yacht can move within Australian waters free of quarantine restrictions. Your animal will spend a minimum of 30 days in quarantine at a Government Quarantine station, the exact period depending on the countries that your yacht has visited in the previous 6 months. In order to qualify for the minimum of 30 days quarantine, it is recommended that in the 6 months prior to import you visit only the following countries (New Zealand, Norfolk Island, Fiji, French Polynesia [includes Tahiti], Guam, Hawaii, Vanuatu, New Caledonia). If other countries have been visited in the previous 6 months, the period in quarantine will be determined based on the country(ies) visited and the rabies vaccination and test status of your animal.

"At the time of arrival in Australia, you will need to present to AQIS acceptable supporting documentation verifying the ports of call in the previous 6 months (ships log, passports, etc, stamped where possible by relevant Port authorities).

"Surveillance of pets on visiting yachts is a labor intensive operation for both AQIS and the yacht owner. The longer the yachts are maintained under quarantine restrictions, the greater the risk of a breach of quarantine integrity.

"Yachts with pets that are intending import should be encouraged to proceed ASAP, to minimize the surveillance responsibility for AQIS and to limit problems associated with managing yachts with pets aboard. If extended quarantine periods are mandated, owners may choose to reject the import option, and maintain pets aboard yachts with extended periods of "Master's Notices." The quarantine period should be set so as to maintain quarantine integrity but encourage owners to import animals at the earliest opportunity. Skippers should be advised of the AQIS inspection charges for maintenance of animals under quarantine surveillance aboard visiting yachts. All decisions regarding period of quarantine must be based on valid ships log or equivalent documentation sighted and accepted by a Quarantine Officer. If the supporting documentation is inadequate, a longer quarantine period may be imposed. It is not necessary to attempt to establish whether animals have remained aboard yachts during their visits to other countries prior to arrival in Australia, as the evidence will not be absolute and will not advance the cause as far as health status of the animal is concerned.

"Visits during last 6 months include only Category 1 countries (New Zealand or Norfolk Island):

- If animal(s) left New Zealand with a New Zealand MAF Health Certificate, animal may be released with Quarantine Entry only (consult AQIS veterinarian if any obvious health concerns);
- if animal(s) did not leave New Zealand with a MAF Health Certificate, animal may be released with Quarantine Entry upon inspection by an AQIS veterinary officer;
- if port of origin is Norfolk Island only, an Import Permit is required before animal can be released with Quarantine Entry.

"Visits during last 6 months include only Category 2 or 3 (+/–Category 1) countries:

- if ports of origin within last 30 days are Category 1 or 2 countries only, animal(s) will qualify for minimum of 30 days PAQ;
- if ports of origin within the last 30 days include a Category 3 country, animal will qualify for 30 days plus an additional 30 minus X days quarantine, X to be calculated as the days spent en route from the Category 3 country to Australia (this effectively allows animals ex Category 3 countries to perform up to the first 30 days of the prescribed 60 days quarantine aboard the yacht in transit).

"Visits during last 6 months include only Category 4 (+/–Category 1,2 or 3) countries:

- If animal(s) are microchipped, are vaccinated against rabies and have a valid, endorsed RNATT result, PAQ period will be determined as per current conditions for import directly from Category 4 countries (i.e. minimum of 30 days up to 120 days depending on date of RNATT sample, assuming at least 60 days elapsed since RNATT).
- If animals do not have valid, endorsed RNATT result, animals will not be permitted import until 6 months after last visit to

Category 4 or non-approved country, after which time the minimum 30 days PAQ applies.

"Visits include Non-Approved countries within last 6 months:

• Animals will not be permitted import until 6 months elapsed since last visit to non-approved country, after which time the minimum 30 days PAQ applies.

"Transport ex yacht to PAQ

Arrangements must be made for movement of the animal(s) from the yacht to the quarantine facility under AQIS control.

"Testing during PAQ

With the exception of animals originating in New Zealand, an Import Permit is required for all imports ex yachts. All dogs imported ex yachts (except those from New Zealand or Norfolk Island) will be tested during PAQ in Australia for Leptospira canicola, Brucella canis and Ehrlichia canis, at the owner's expense, and will not be eligible for release from quarantine until they comply with AQIS conditions for import.

"Advanced Notice of Yachts arrival:

Where intending yacht visitors make contact with AQIS well in advance of the intended arrival date in Australia, skippers should be encouraged to visit only Category 2 or 3 countries in the last 6 months, and Category 3 countries at least 30 days prior to arrival in Australia. Also emphasise with skippers the importance of having Port Authorities sign, date and stamp a ship's log in order to assist AQIS in verifying the dates of visiting those countries."

The forms and worksheets for Australia are in the appendix along with a list of ports with AQIS stations. There are telephone numbers for the stations, also. As you can see, there is an effort on the part of the government to give you advance notice and to cooperate in making the quarantine as brief as possible. Although regulations in the Pacific are particularly strict, there is recognition of the need to encourage your visit and enjoyment of the country. The Australians encourage you to visit countries that they consider better risks before coming to Australia thereby shortening the length of quarantine for your pet.

New Zealand

New Zealand permits importation without quarantine of cats or dogs from Australia, Hawaii, Republic of Ireland, Singapore, and the United Kingdom. The importation is subject to an MAF Import Health Certificate, which is issued by the immigration office. The website is listed in the appendix.

We did not find provision for a self-imposed quarantine on the boat as is permitted in Australia. Therefore, if you bring a pet from other than the five countries listed, expect to have at least a 30-day quarantine after complying with the advance certification procedures. You may find that if you voyage to New Zealand via Tonga—a common route for cruisers—without advance preparation you might incur as much as 120 days of quarantine.

Again, if you plan to be in a country with strict regulations, it is important to make contact well in advance, so that you can be prepared to cope with the regulations. Many cruisers have made the mistake of assuming that cats aren't required to meet the rabies laws. In some countries, the rules may be lax, but it is a mistake to ignore them.

Philippines

In the Philippines, we spent our time anchored out so were not faced with the problem of taking a pet ashore. We did learn an interesting lesson from another boat of Australian registry. The family had been cruising for some time. The daughters were returning to Australia to resume school. While in the Philippines they had adopted a lovely calico cat. When the family prepared to fly home, they did not take the cat. It wasn't clear whether they had protected the cat with shots or not, but they were advised that the cat would have to serve maximum quarantine, 120-days, when they arrived in Australia. In lieu of taking the cat, they left it aboard their boat, moored in the anchorage.

We arrived several months after their departure for Australia. They had not returned in the time that their fellow cruisers assumed they would. A local "boat boy" was feeding the cat and looking after the boat. Clearly, the system had broken down. The cat was lonely, mal-

FOREIGN TRAVEL 🐾 153

nourished, and living in filth. If we happened to pass close by in our dinghy, the cat would jump up on the bow roller and cry plaintively. This apparently abandoned pet upset all of the cruisers.

Finally, a Canadian single-hander took the cat aboard his boat. He thought that it might be happier with care, and he planned to return the cat to the owners upon their return. His good deed lasted for a few days, and then he returned the cat to its home. He said that the cat was so neurotic it sat and cried. Even when it was fed, petted, or just wandering about the boat, it cried constantly.

A few more weeks passed and the owners returned to their boat. By this time, many of the cruisers were very angry about the treatment of the cat, and said so. The owners explained that they never intended to be away so long, they had paid for the cat's care, and they were upset by our reception. They planned to leave again. Before they left, the cat disappeared. I don't know if they gave it away or if it was kidnapped. My reaction was that whatever happened, it was probably an improvement for the cat.

In all of the Philippines, visiting numerous ports, our cat was never an issue. We saw very few pets except among other cruisers or landed expatriates. The islands do have rabies. They also have a population that for the most part can't afford luxuries such as companion pets. If you plan to cruise in the Philippines, be sure that your pet has all the necessary inoculations, and keep your pet in your possession at all times. As our friend Mary described in her letter in the previous chapter, the veterinarians didn't seem competent. She felt veterinary training was inadequate to cope with companion pets.

Hong Kong

After several months in Hong Kong, we discovered that there were rules about pets. We were on a mooring, as are almost all cruisers, and had checked in by visiting the offices in the central district. The officials never visited our boat, and no one asked about pets. We planned to visit nearby Macao via ferry, as the surrounding waters were too shallow for our eight-foot draft. I asked at the yacht club if they knew of a place to board our cat for a few days. They didn't know, but the veterinarian in the next building would certainly have an answer.

I contacted the veterinarian who gave me the telephone number for a cattery. Then I discovered there were rules about pets. Although our cat was current with rabies shots, I hadn't bothered with other felines shots. They told me that before I could bring a foreign cat to their premises a veterinarian had to examine him and certify he had current shots. I called the veterinarian back for an appointment. The cattery accepted Boca, and he was isolated but well cared for the few days we were gone. When the cattery delivered Boca to the dock, we talked about entry requirements.

All dogs must be certified rabies free and have a microchip. Any dog without a microchip will be euthanized. Owners have until a dog is six-months old to comply. There were no rules for cats, but the local veterinary association had recommended that cats be treated in the same manner. The owner of the cattery advised that they put foreign cats in isolation unless they were from Australia or New Zealand. I realized as the only Americans, no one thought that our situation might be different from the other cruisers. We were never told that there was a government enforced quarantine period.

Japan

We spent more than a year in Japan. Most of our stops were in marinas. At every port, officials boarded us. Boca greeted all of those officials whether they wanted to be or not. He soon learned that he was "neko-chan," the cat. There was never an inkling that rules about pets existed for cruisers.

In Japan, we had to leave every 90 days to renew our visas. The first time, a local veterinary asked to be honored by taking care of Boca. We have learned that no one can match the hospitality that is deeply ingrained in that culture. The price for honoring the veterinarian was to permit pictures of Boca and us with the veterinarian. At each stop, we encountered people who arranged cat care, brought special cat food, and adored our pet.

We finally asked a friend who raises yellow Labradors about the rules in Japan. He said the rules are very strict for dogs. His dogs travel to be shown in other countries and must have certificates, shots, and blood tests. Knowing that Japan is included in the PETS law in Great Britain, we must assume that Japan is strict. I questioned why there appeared to be no rules for cats. Whether his explanation is accurate or not, is unclear to me. He said that the "Kanji," the Chinese characters that are part of the Japanese written language, for rabies translates as "mad dog disease," and perhaps that is why cats are not subject to the rules.

Another explanation is that the cat is a type of deity referred to as "Maneki-neko." I know you have seen the statues of the cat with the uplifted paw in stores and restaurants. Whatever the truth is about cats, clearly there is an unwritten inequity in Japan.

Russia

Despite the most difficult and trying bureaucracy we have ever encountered, Boca was not a problem. We understand there are stringent rules, but there was no indication of them in eastern Russia when we entered at Nahodka, on the Pacific Coast. Officials filled our boat for hours. We had spent months acquiring the proper visas and sponsorship papers. We had a sponsor on the docks when we arrived to serve as translator.

Boca did his best to be noticed by walking all over the papers, the briefcases, and the inspectors. He was given a few hostile stares and a share of chin scratches. His presence was never questioned. When we moored next to a beautiful racing yacht at the Antares Yacht Club, the skipper and crew had to see our cat. Their boat was Bagira, a storybook black leopard, with a huge graphic of the cat on the hull. They wanted our cat as their mascot. No deal!

United States

I have heard rumors that returning with your pet is difficult. We never have had trouble, but I decided to ask friends who come and go every year. They cruise in the Caribbean and then return to San Diego each summer. This is what Don told me about bringing Tristan home this last time.

"Returning to the States is not a problem. Coming through Puerto Rico this past season, there were long lines waiting to clear, but upon seeing us dragging our bags, pushing the cart, and walking the dog, they waved us through and forgot to grab our declaration. I suppose we'll be arrested next time."

We tried to check back in to the USA in Adak, Dutch Harbor (immigration only), Kodiak, and finally succeeded in telephoning in our arrival at Sitka. No one ever asked about a pet. The USCG finally boarded us at Cape Omaney, but they were interested in PFDs, papers, and destinations. Boca slept through the whole experience after he had checked out the officers.

We expect the verification of rabies vaccinations as a requirement whenever we cross the US border with a pet. Others tell us, they are always asked. Before you leave home, call or check the website listed in the appendix for US Customs and the USDA.

Veterinary Care

Clearly as you travel from country to country, you will need to make contact with a local veterinarian before checking out and going to your next port. Generally, you will find other cruisers who have had dealings with a local veterinarian and can make a recommendation. The level of skill varies from country to country so be as selective as possible. If you are not competent in the local language, make sure the veterinarian you select speaks your language. Take all of the documents verifying your pet's vaccination history.

Traveling on land with your pet may prove difficult. Take your cat or small dog in a carrier so that you can use a taxi or bus. If you have a large dog, plan to walk or find a taxi driver who will allow you to bring the dog in the car. If you have a particularly large dog, you may be required to muzzle it. Veterinary facilities are not elegant, and normally don't offer separate waiting rooms for cats and dogs. In some countries, you may need to take ferries, buses, trucks, and cabs for several hours to reach a veterinarian. On the island of Mindoro in the Philippines, we were two hours from the veterinarian. It required a dinghy ride from the boat to the ferry dock, 45–60 minutes on the ferry, 30 minutes in a jeepney (an enclosed truck with no head room and wooden seats), and another 30 minutes on foot.

In some areas, you will find conditions very primitive. It may mean for you that you should try to care for your pet on your own. If you

Finding a qualified vet in a foreign country requires effort and time.

have any doubt about conditions or expertise, ask for information and permission to examine the premises. It is important that you use the utmost tact and courtesy in seeking permission. Generally, we found foreign veterinary services were eager to show us their facilities and other patients. Even when other cruisers made recommendations, we attempted to examine the facilities in advance.

Most countries that have been marginal economically are still struggling to meet the needs of pet owners. In some countries, veterinary care is available for large animals that are an economic resource. Care for cows, oxen, horses, camels, and even elephants, is available in countries that don't have small pet facilities. On the other hand, in those countries where pet ownership is a status symbol, it can be very expensive.

A friend helped me to check on several veterinary boarding catteries in Asia. Some of the facilities charged as much as a hotel. I was lucky that my friend was a local and negotiated a lower price.

Taking your pet into another country can be an adventure. Remember that you will be faced with regulations, expenses, and possibly ignorance. Make sure that you are prepared to cope with problems including separation and illness.

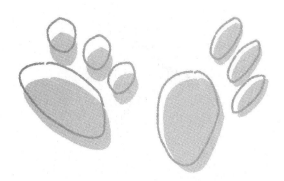

Epilog

When we suffer the loss of a pet, we often think that we can't go through it again. When our first black cat, Zorba, disappeared in Yugoslavia, we searched and cried. We walked the paths on the beach, dove in cold water, and stopped everyone we encountered. No one had seen our cat. We didn't know how important he had become to us until he disappeared.

A few weeks later, we returned to our boat after a shopping excursion in town. On the cabin top, in the shade of the dinghy, the spot Zorba always watched from, we found a small, dirty white kitten. We thought hard but agreed it was too soon. We took the kitten to the marina office and they were delighted.

Nearly two years passed before we adopted another kitten. Foxy, like Zorba, was black. They were nearly identical in body shape and voice. Fearless and vocal, Foxy was an ideal replacement. From New York he made the trip through the Great Lakes, down the Mississippi, across the Gulf, and finally through the Panama Canal and back to the US.

Unfortunately, our home marina refused to let us have a pet. Fortunately, Foxy found a home with our family in the foothills. He flourishes there today enjoying the rush of chasing ducks and peacocks. We gave him up with sadness but know he is happy.

Boca has been with us the longest. We have worked hard to make his cruising life a happy one. It has been expensive at times. It has been frightening to deal with his health problems. It has been frustrating to arrange his care so that we can take trips of duration away from the boat. There are nights when he insists upon sleeping between us in an already crowded bunk. It is his way of proving that he is part of the family.

Think seriously about your pet before taking him aboard. He is a living creature and you must be prepared to accept the responsibility of his existence everyday. After all, he is dependent on you and can only repay with love and affection.

APPENDIX A
Product and
Organization Websites

BoatU.S.	www.boatus.com/pets
Buddy Bowl: spill proof bowls	www.buddybowl.com
Comfort Lift for dogs	www.drsfostersmith.com
Dog Biscuit Mix	www.kingarthurflour.com
Eat-n-neat pet food dispensers	www.eatneat.com
Eliminate on Command Dr. Marjorie L. Smith	www.seaworthy.com
microchip identification	www.avidid.com www.homeagainid.com
Neo Paws: boots, flotation, rainwear	www.neo-paw.com
PetSTEP Ramp/Utility Table	www.petstep.com
Positive Pet Deodorant	www.odorless.com
Restraining harness: VestHarness	www.caninefriendly.com
Ruff Wear: flotation and boots for pets	www.ruffwear.com
Stearns Inc.: flotation for pets	www.stearnsinc.com
UHT Milk	www.netgrocer.com
Waterhole from Dog Outfitters also carries Nilodor	www.dogsoutfitter.com

APPENDIX B
Sources for Quarantine Information/Regulations

United States of America

US Customs Service – www.customs.gov/travel/
US Department of Agriculture – www.aphis.usda.gov

Great Britain

PETS, the travel regulations for Great Britain – www.defra.gov.uk
   Letter re quarantine laws in the UK:

Thank you for your recent enquiry regarding the inclusion of the United States of America into the Pet Travel Scheme.

   When it announced the introduction of PETS, the Government said those pets from non-qualifying countries such as the US and Canada would continue to be subject to quarantine. However, the Government did indicate that it would look again at the position for these two countries.

   We have agreed in principle to extend PETS to North America. The independent scientific assessment of the risk of importing rabies if the Pet Travel Scheme was extended to North America has proved encouraging. The results of that work suggest that extending the Pet Travel Scheme (PETS) to North America would not significantly increase the risk of importing rabies compared to the current risk under PETS. However, a peer review of the assessment identified a need to clarify some details about the model on which it was based.

   It is vital that we have a clear and solid scientific basis on which to base our decision on this matter and we cannot make a final decision until we are confident that the necessary evidence on the risk of importing rabies is clear. Further work has been commissioned to produce this. This work is due to be completed by the autumn.

We recognise that this will mean a small delay in making our final decision on an extension to North America. We also need to continue our discussions with the European Commission on how pets from North America will be treated under the new Regulation covering pet movements within and into the Community. This is likely to come into force late next year.

(Please note that cats and dogs that come to the UK from a country that is not in the Pet Travel Scheme have to spend six months in quarantine. More information about booking an animal into quarantine premises (including a list of premises) and obtaining an import license can be found on our website www.defra.gov.uk/animalh/quarantine or by calling the quarantine section +44 (0)20 7904 6222.)

As soon as we are in a position to make a further announcement, we will do so but this is not likely until the autumn.

In anticipation of the US/Canada becoming a qualifying country for the Scheme some pet owners in the US/Canada are preparing their cats and dogs under the existing PETS criteria. Information on the requirements for animals entering the UK under the Scheme from the current qualifying Long Haul countries such as micro-chipping, vaccination, blood testing, the six-month wait and seals on containers is included in the attached factsheet. Please note that the pet must be at least three months old and be vaccinated, after the microchip has been inserted, with an approved inactivated adjuvanted vaccine, before being blood tested.

To qualify for PETS, an animal must be first fitted with a microchip as a permanent record of identity. Then vaccinated against rabies and then blood tested. Your animal will then be eligible for entry into the UK without quarantine six-months after the date the blood sample was taken. This however is dependant on the U.S becoming a qualifying country for the purposes of the Pet Travel Scheme.

Paragraph 4 in the Fact Sheet ' The blood test' mentions DEFRA recognised laboratories. There is now a recognised laboratory in the US:

KSU Rabies Laboratory
Mosier Hall
1800 Denison Ave
Kansas State University
Manhattan KS 66506-5600
Phone/Fax: (785) 532-4298

The veterinarian should check on the sample submission procedures with the lab. I should emphasise that animals being prepared in a qualifying country to enter the UK under the Scheme have a six-month waiting period from the date of a blood sample being taken which yielded a successful test result. In addition once you have prepared your pet for the Scheme you must maintain the specified rabies vaccination programme to avoid a further blood test and six month wait.

Any change on the status of North America with regard to the Scheme will be posted on our website www.defra.gov.uk/animalh/quarantine as soon as the information becomes available.

Dependant on the U.S and Canada becoming qualifying countries for the Pet Travel Scheme. One of the criteria for entry into the UK once all the procedures have been met is that the animal arrives into the UK by means of an approved carrier.

The interpretation of an approved "carrier" means any undertaking carrying goods or passengers for hire by land,sea or air.

Ultimately, participation in the Scheme is a commercial decision by the carriers, if they wish to participate a system of auditing and inspection of carriers and their facilities will be put into place. These checks will provide a safeguard to ensure that carriers comply fully with prescribed procedures.

Therefore entry into the UK with animals is not permitted by means of a private vessel.

If you would like to receive an information pack or discuss any of the procedures outlined above in more detail please do not hesitate to contact me directly.

Yours sincerely

Jim Gray
PET TRAVEL SCHEME
ANIMAL IDENTIFICATION AND INTERNATIONAL TRADE TEAM

News Release

PETS TRAVEL SCHEME EXTENDED TO USA AND CANADA

The successful PETS Travel Scheme is to be extended to dogs and cats from the United States and Canada, Animal Health Minister Elliot Morley announced today.

From 11 December, people coming to this country from the USA and Canada will be able to bring their vaccinated pets without having to put them into six months quarantine. However, until an approved route from North America is available and official certification agreed, animals will have to go into short stay quarantine, usually only for two to three days, whilst the microchip and paperwork are checked.

Announcing the extension to North America, Elliot Morley said:

"I am proud to be associated with the Pet Travel Scheme. Since we introduced the Scheme in February 2000 over 75,000 dogs and cats from Europe and rabies-free islands have used the Scheme to enter the UK without having to go into six months quarantine.

"When we introduced the Scheme we recognised that there was significant demand from people in the USA and Canada, and indeed UK travellers, for those two countries to be included in the Scheme. We were cautious about doing so, but did undertake to consider again whether or not to include these countries in the Scheme. We have now done this.

"We have carried out several scientific assessments of the risk of importing rabies if the Pet Travel Scheme was extended to USA and Canada. Both these assessments concluded that the risk of importing rabies into the UK by extending the Pet Travel Scheme to the USA and Canada was low.

"I know that some people feel that we have been too cautious in our approach to including the USA and Canada in our Pet Travel Scheme. But we were not prepared to take such a significant step until we were sure, on a sound scientific basis, that there would be no significant increase in the risks of importing rabies if the Scheme was extended to those countries.

"We now have this assurance and I am therefore very pleased to announce that the Government has decided to extend the Pet Travel Scheme to USA and Canada.

"Because of the many close links between our countries many people in the USA and Canada have the opportunity to come and live and work in the UK. But some refuse because they cannot bear to be separated from their cats or dogs for the six months they must stay in quarantine.

"I am delighted to say that the legislation giving effect to this change has been laid before Parliament today and will come into force on Wednesday 11 December. From that date, dogs and cats from the USA and Canada which meet the requirements of the Pet Travel Scheme will be able to enter the UK without going into quarantine for six months.

"I would also like to take this opportunity to stress that all the conditions applying to the Pet Travel Scheme must be complied with if an animal is to avoid six months quarantine. We have prepared explanatory leaflets for pet owners and US and Canadian vets. These are available from my Department and are on our Website."

Discussions with airlines for approval of routes into England and with the authorities in the USA and Canada about appropriate certification to accompany such animals continue. Until these are in place, qualifying animals will have to go into quarantine for a few days until it is confirmed that they do meet fully the requirements of the Pet Travel Scheme. If they do then they will be released from quarantine as quickly as possible.

The UK has been free from rabies for many years and wishes to remain so. The Pet Travel Scheme rules are strictly applied; it is the responsibility of the pet owner to make sure their animal meets all the conditions of the Scheme and that the owner has all the documentation to prove this. Travellers from the USA and Canada must bring their documentation with them.

In the UK and Europe most microchips and scanners comply with ISO Standards. The USA and Canada have different microchips. Owners of animals identified with non-ISO microchips may experience some difficulties in demonstrating that their animal has been microchipped. Such owners are advised to provide their own scanner.

Trinidad/Tobago

Current quarantine information – www.boatersenterpise.com

Hawaii

State of Hawaii, Department of Agriculture Division of Animal Industry 99-941 Halawa Valley Street Aiea, Hawaii 96701-3246 Tel: (808) 483-7100 Fax: (808) 483-7110 30-DAY PRE-ARRIVAL REQUIREMENTS - www.hawaiiag.org/hdoa/ai_aqs_info.htm

New Zealand

New Zealand Pet Quarantine Information - www.nzimmigration.com/pets

General

Blaine & Janet Parks' website with quarantine information – www.sailcharbonneau.com

Australia

QUARANTINE REQUIREMENTS FOR THE IMPORTATION OF CATS AND DOGS FROM APPROVED COUNTRIES IN WHICH RABIES IS ABSENT OR WELL CONTROLLED

MINIMUM 30 DAYS QUARANTINE IN AUSTRALIA

The list of countries in this category ("Appendix 1") is subject to change. The most current information including country lists can be obtained via the Internet at www.aqis.gov.au or by e-mail at animalimp@aqis.gov.au or by ph +612 6272 4454 or by fax +612 6272 3110

THE PROCESS FOR IMPORTING YOUR CAT OR DOG IS SUMMARISED BELOW. DETAILS OF IMPORT REQUIREMENTS ARE CONTAINED IN STEPS 1-20. THESE STEPS MUST BE COMPLETED PRIOR TO IMPORTING YOUR PET. In most cases these steps proceed in the order specified.

SUMMARY
All animals entering Australia require a permit to import, issued by AQIS. To obtain a permit to import, an application ("Appendix 4") must be completed and returned to the quarantine station of your choice. Your application must include your pet's microchip number. Section 7 of your application form must be completed, signed and stamped by an Official Veterinarian. The permit to import that will be returned to you defines additional import requirements. These additional requirements include tests, treatments and inspections that must be completed prior to export. AQIS accepts that these requirements have been completed satisfactorily when certified on Veterinary Certificates A and B provided with the permit to import. The original permit to import, original Veterinary Certificates A and B, and the required laboratory reports and vaccination certificates must accompany your pet to Australia. Your pet and all accompanying documents must be linked unequivocally by means of your pet's microchip number which must also be included on Veterinary Certificate A and B and the laboratory reports. The steps below provide additional information for completing the entire process.

STEP 1: GENERAL ELIGIBILITY   *check once completed* ____
Time Frame: Confirm eligibility before proceeding.
Residency
> Dogs and cats must have been continuously living in the country of export for a minimum of 6 months immediately prior to shipment, or since direct importation from Australia (please see the section on "Dogs and cats returning to Australia after less than 6 months residency in country of export" before proceeding).
>
> The animal must not have been under quarantine restrictions in the 30 days prior to export.
>
> AQIS may allow the importation of dogs and cats from the European Union that have not completed 6 months residency in the country of export. The animal(s) must have been continuously resident for the 6 months prior to export in AQIS approved European Union countries. Documentation to support residency status must be provided to the Official Veterinarian endorsing Veterinary Certificates A and B.

Age
> Animals must be more than six (6) months old at time of export.

Pregnancy
> Animals must not be more than 6 weeks pregnant, nor be suckling young at time of export.

Dangerous Breeds
> Dogs of the following breeds are not eligible for importation into Australia:
> - dogo Argentino;
> - fila Brazileiro;
> - Japanese tosa;
> - Pit bull terrier or American pit bull;
> - Domestic animal hybrids such as with wolves or Bengal cats are not eligible for export to Australia, unless they are proven to be 5th generation or more away from any pure-bred ancestor. Please contact Wildlife Permits and Enforcement Section, Environment Australia on 02 6274 1111 for further information.

STEP 2: CHECK THE DATE OF LAST RABIES VACCINATION
N.B. CATS *AND* DOGS   *check once completed* ____
Time Frame: Check dates immediately. Your dog or cat must be vaccinated <u>preferably 6 months prior to export</u> and not more than 1 year prior to export.

Note: The vaccination date may indirectly determine the amount of time your animal has to spend in quarantine in Australia. See the table in step 5 for advice.

Ensure the date of last rabies vaccination is <u>within 12 months of the date of export</u> to Australia. If not, arrange for the dog or cat to be vaccinated/ revaccinated with an approved inactivated rabies vaccine according to a or b.

a) Primovaccination

The animal must be at least 3 months old at the time of the first vaccination. The vaccination must be given between 12 months and 90 days prior to export.

b) Subsequent Vaccinations

Where the primovaccination or subsequent vaccinations were given more than 12 months prior to the date of export a booster vaccination must be given. This booster must be given within 12 months prior to export.

The primovaccination certificate, or the most current rabies vaccination booster certificate must be presented to the Official Veterinarian when completing Section 7 of the application form.

STEP 3: MICROCHIP CAT OR DOG   *check once completed* ____
Time Frame: Before Step 5

Dogs and cats must be identified by a microchip that can be read by an Avid â, Trovanâ, Destronâ or other ISO compatible reader. The microchip must be implanted before <u>any</u> testing takes place.

STEP 4: FIND A "REGISTERED" VETERINARIAN, AN "OFFICIAL (GOVERNMENT) VETERINARIAN" AND A " GOVERNMENT APPROVED LABORATORY."   *check once completed* ____
Time frame: Immediately, or before step 5.

A registered (licensed) veterinarian has completed a tertiary degree to become a veterinarian and has been registered by either a state or federal government body; enabling them to work in a veterinary practice. In some countries a registered veterinarian can do most of the veterinary work for export eg. blood collecting, vaccinations. In other countries veterinarians must be government approved to perform export work.

The USA requires that only registered veterinarians who are also accredited by the United States Department of Agriculture (USDA) prepare animals for export. Ensure that you contact a USDA-accredited veterinarian to prepare your pet for import to Australia. In the USA most registered (licensed) veterinarians are also USDA accredited.

An "Official Veterinarian" is a government officer employed by the government veterinarian administration (eg USDA) in the exporting country. Official Veterinarians generally do not work in private practice. Official Veterinarians are able to sign certificates on behalf of the government's veterinary administration.

A registered (licensed) or accredited veterinarian will prepare your pet for export to Australia and fill in the details of this preparation on Veterinary Certificate A. An Official Veterinarian must endorse Veterinary Certificate A and complete Veterinary Certificate B. The Official Veterinarian must also complete, sign and stamp Section 7 of your application form before it can be forwarded to AQIS.

Veterinary Certificates A and B must be completed in English and where necessary in a language understood by the Official Veterinarian.

"Government approved laboratories" are approved by the government veterinary service for testing samples from animals destined for export. AQIS allows the use of Government approved laboratories in countries other than the country of export. If necessary the Australian Animal Health Laboratory (AAHL) can do all testing for you. Fax: 613 5227 5555 Ph: 613 5227 5329

To locate appropriate veterinarians and laboratories, contact the government quarantine, agriculture or food departments in the country of export. Alternatively, contact AQIS.

ADDITIONAL TESTING REQUIREMENTS FOR DOGS AND CATS FROM MALAYSIA ONLY   *check once completed* ____
Time frame: Within 45 days prior to export.

All dogs and cats from Malaysia must be tested for Nipah virus by the Serum Neutralisation test at AAHL, Victoria, on a blood sample collected within 45 days prior to export, with negative results.
Please retain this laboratory report.

STEP 5: RABIES NEUTRALISING
ANTIBODY TITRE TEST (RNATT)   *check once completed* ____
Time frame: Three to four weeks after the rabies vaccination and at least 60 days prior to import

Note: The date that the blood is drawn for the RNATT will determine the amount of time your pet must stay in quarantine in Australia. One hundred and eighty (180) days must elapse between the date that the blood was taken for the RNAT test (with a satisfactory result) and the date your pet is released from quarantine in Australia. Keep in mind that your pet must spend at least 30 days in a quarantine kennel in Australia regardless of when the blood was taken for the RNATT test. This means that if you want your pets to be quarantined in Australia for the minimum amount of time (30 days), blood for the RNAT test must be taken at least 150 days prior to the export of your pet.

Collection of sample for RNATT	Minimum quarantine period
150 days or more prior to arrival in Australia	30 days
135 days prior to arrival in Australia	45 days
120 days prior to arrival in Australia	60 days
90 days prior to arrival in Australia	90 days
65 days prior to arrival in Australia	115 days

Additionally, your pet will not be eligible for entry into Australia if it has not completed the following minimum requirements:

Minimum period between rabies primovaccination and export to Australia	90 days
Minimum period between blood collection for RNATT and export to Australia	60 days

Arrange for a registered (licensed) or accredited veterinarian to draw a blood sample for the RNATT. This test will determine the rabies antibody status of your cat or dog and confirm that the rabies vaccination was successful. AQIS recommends that you wait approximately 3 -4 weeks from the date of the last rabies vaccination before your veterinarian collects the blood. This enables your pet to produce sufficient antibodies to record a positive result.

A government-approved laboratory must carry out testing. The RNATT must result in a titre of at least 0.5 IU/ml. Your cat or dogs microchip number must be used to identify the blood samples and must appear on the laboratory report. If a result of less than 0.5 IU/ml is obtained you must re-vaccinate your pet and repeat the process.

The RNATT report must be presented to an Official Veterinarian when completing Section 7 of the application form. A copy of the RNATT report must be submitted with your application for an Import Permit.

Please note that if the export of your pet is delayed you will have to repeat the RNATT test within 12 months of the original test. If the RNATT test expires (i.e. the time period between tests is greater than 12 months) your pet will have to begin the process again and endure the long waiting periods above. If the RNATT test is repeated within the twelve months your pet is considered to have continuous protection against rabies. He/she will not have to go back to the beginning of the process again.

STEP 6: APPLY FOR A PERMIT TO IMPORT   *check once completed* ____
Time frame: At least 2 months prior to export

Your pet will not be allowed to enter Australia without a valid AQIS permit to import. Pets that arrive without a permit will be re-exported immediately to the country of origin, or may be destroyed.

Fill out the application form attached. Please ensure that you have done the following.

- Included payment (Australian dollars) for permit to import ("Appendix 5") in the form of a cheque, or credit card details and signature, made out to "The Collector Of Public Monies AQIS". The Animal Quarantine Fee Schedule for dogs and cats is at ("Appendix 3").
- Section 7 of the application form has been complete, signed and stamped by an Official Veterinarian.
- Attached a copy of the RNATT report

The application form must be sent to the quarantine station in which your pet is to undergo post-entry quarantine. The list of quarantine stations can be found in Appendix 2.

STEP 7: PERMIT TO IMPORT   *check once completed* ____
Time Frame: The permit will be posted to you immediately following approval of your application by AQIS. Permits will be posted to the "exporter" (and the "shipper" where required) as detailed in the application form.

The permit includes Veterinary Certificates A and B. These contain details of additional requirements that must be completed prior to the export of your pet. This information sheet will also take you through the steps required to complete the Veterinary Certificates.

You should note that the permit is valid for 6 months only, and will be tailored around your pets expected date of arrival in Australia. The original Import Permit must be sent with your pet to Australia.

STEP 8: COMMENCE
TRAVEL ARRANGEMENTS   *check once completed* ____
    Time frame: As soon as you have received the import permit from AQIS.
    Some airlines will not book travel until testing is completed. However AQIS advises you to contact airlines as soon as the permit to import is received.

    Your pet can only come into Australia through the following airports, Kingsford Smith Airport in Sydney (New South Wales), or Tullamarine Airport in Melbourne (Victoria), or Perth Airport in Perth (Western Australia). Other entry points can only be used with the prior consent of AQIS.
    AQIS does not place any restrictions on the airline you choose to use. However your pet must travel as "Manifested Cargo", not in the cabin, in an International Air Transport Association (IATA) approved container for dogs and cats. Strict compliance with container specifications is vital for the safe and secure transport of your animal. Problems will occur if your pet can escape from this container or if any part of its body (nose/limbs/tail) can protrude. Your airline can help you with these requirements.
    It may be cheaper to transport your pet if you travel on the same flight.
    During transport to Australia pets may transit in all countries (AQIS approved or not). Trans-shipment (change aircraft or vessel) is permitted in all countries except through Malaysia. Trans-shipment is not permitted through Malaysia. AQIS strongly advises booking direct flights due to health and welfare concerns, eg pets missing connecting flights and remaining in airports for extended periods.

    Trans-shipment may also require approval from the quarantine authority in the country of trans-shipment.
    If you are not able to organise travel yourself there are animal transport agents in most countries who can make arrangements on your behalf.

    Please note you will be charged an additional fee of $25 if your pet arrives in Australia outside business hours (8:00am - 4:00 pm). You are also required to seek the approval of the relevant quarantine station for after hour's pick-ups, from the airport, prior to import.

The Australian Government accepts no responsibility for animals that escape en route, and all transport costs are at the expense of the importer.

STEP 9: GENERAL VACCINATIONS *check once completed* ___
Time frame: Between 12 months and 14 days prior to export.

Vaccinations must be valid for the entire period spent in quarantine in Australia. If vaccinations expire prior to your pet's release from quarantine they may be re-vaccinated at the owners expense.

Dogs must be vaccinated against distemper, infectious hepatitis, canine parvovirus (parvo), *Bordetella bronchiseptica* (kennel cough) and para-influenza. Dogs may be vaccinated for kennel cough on arrival in Australia at the owners expense.

Vaccinations against *Leptospira interrogans*.var. *canicola* are not required for export to Australia and is therefore optional. Vaccination against Leptospirosis may cause a blood titre rise. The animal may not meet the test as required in Step 12.

Cats must have been vaccinated against feline enteritis (feline panleucopaenia), rhinotracheitis and calicivirus.

Please retain these vaccination certificates.

DOGS ONLY

STEP 10: DOGS ONLY,
BRUCELLOSIS, EHRLICHIOSIS *check once completed* ___
Time frame: Within 45 days of export.

Note: This step may be undertaken at the same time as Step 12 if required. You will have to complete Step 11 within 24 hours of the collection of the blood for the ehrlichiosis test.

Arrange for a veterinarian to draw blood samples from your dog for brucellosis and ehrlichiosis (tropical canine pancytopaenia) and send to a government-approved laboratory.

Brucellosis: Your dog must be tested for *Brucella canis* infection by serum agglutination test (the use of any other test requires prior written permission from AQIS) on a blood sample collected within 45 days prior to export. The test must produce a negative result (less than 50% agglutination at serum dilution of 1:100). Once blood is collected for this test your dog must not be mated or inseminated until after its arrival in Australia.

Ehrlichiosis: Your dog must be tested for *Ehrlichia canis* infection by the indirect fluorescent antibody test (the use of any other test requires prior written permission from AQIS) on a sample collected within 45 days prior to export. The test must produce a negative result.

Leptospirosis: For dogs vaccinated for Leptospirosis, please read Step 12b.

Please retain these certificates.

Contact AQIS if your dog does not meet the requirements of these tests.

DOGS ONLY

STEP 11: DOGS ONLY
EXTERNAL PARASITES   *check once completed* ____
Time frame: Within 24 hour of collection of blood for ehrlichiosis (Step 10)

Your veterinarian must treat your dog with a long lasting acaricide that is registered for the control of ticks and mites eg Frontline® (active ingredient is fipronil) or Permoxin® (active ingredient is permethrin).

Revolution® is unacceptable as the parasite must bite the animal before the parasite is killed. Revolution® also takes several days after application to reach maximum effectiveness.

Oral products and medicated collars are not satisfactory. Ivermectin® and Macrocyclic lactone products, (oral, injectable or topical) are not satisfactory treatments. Washes and rinses are generally acceptable. The treatment must be repeated according to the manufacturer's instructions in order to prevent infestation with ticks and mites from the first application until export. Dates of treatment will need to be recorded on Veterinary Certificate A.

Re-application of the acaricide will usually have to take place between 2 week and 4 weeks after the first application depending on the manufacturers recommendations. Dates of treatment will need to be recorded on Veterinary Certificate A. Your pet must remain free of external parasites until export.

DOGS ONLY

STEP 12: DOGS ONLY LEPTOSPIROSIS   *check once completed* ____
Time frame: Within 21 days of export

Arrange for a veterinarian to draw blood samples from your dog for
leptospirosis and send to a government-approved laboratory.

Leptospirosis: Your dog must be tested for *Leptospira interrogans*
var. *canicola* by serum agglutination testing, by either a or b.

a) Unvaccinated dogs must be tested within 21 days of export and
must record a negative (less than 50% agglutination at a serum dilution of 1:100) result.

b) Vaccinated dogs may either be tested once within 21 days of
export and record a negative result (as in a) or be tested within 45 days
of export and again not less than 14 days after the first test. When two
tests are performed, both tests should record a result of not more than
1:400, the second test must not show an increase in titre above the first
test. Confirmation that the dog has been vaccinated against leptospirosis must appear on the Veterinary Certificate.

Please retain these reports.

Contact AQIS if your dog does not meet the requirements of this
test.

STEP 13: BOOK PRE FLIGHT INSPECTION   *check once completed* ____
Time Frame: As soon as testing is completed.

The pre-flight examination of your pet, which includes completion of
Veterinary Certificate A, must take place within 48 hours prior to departure by a registered (licensed) or accredited (USA) or Official Veterinarian in the country of export. If the animal is from the USA, book
pre-export inspection of animal with the USDA (located at LA airport
or at regional locations).

STEP 14: INTERNAL PARASITE TREATMENT   *check once completed* ____
Time frame: Within 14 days of travel.

Arrange for a veterinarian to treat your cat or dog for internal parasites
with an anthelmintic effective against nematodes and cestodes eg Drontal
®. The active ingredient and the dose rate must be recorded on Veterinary
Certificate A.

DOGS WHICH HAVE LIVED IN AFRICA ONLY

STEP 15: DOGS THAT HAVE LIVED IN AFRICA
ONLY BABESIOSIS   *check once completed* ____
Time frame: Between 5-3 days prior to export.

Dogs must be treated with imidocarb dipropionate (Forray-65®, by Hoechst) or (Imizol® by Coopers) at a rate of 7.5mg per Kg body weight by subcutaneous injection. Details must be recorded on Veterinary Certificate A.

CATS ONLY

STEP 16: CATS ONLY EXTERNAL
PARASITE TREATMENT   *check once completed* ____
Time frame: Within 96 hours of export

Give single treatment for external parasites using a long acting product effective against ticks, mites and fleas. Oral products and insecticide collars are not satisfactory. Washes and rinses are generally acceptable.
    The date on which this treatment was applied must be recorded on Veterinary Certificate A.

DOGS ONLY

STEP 17: FLEA BATH FOR DOGS   *check once completed* ____
Time frame: Approximately 48 hours before export

If the external parasite treatment commenced in Step 11 was not effective for fleas, your dog should be treated for fleas now.

STEP 18: COMPLETION OF VETERINARY CERTIFICATE A,
INCLUDING PRE-EXPORT INSPECTION   *check once completed* ____
Time frame: Within 48 hours of the departure time
    Please read over Veterinary Certificate A prior to the appointment. Your pet will have to be presented for inspection.
    Veterinary Certificate A is to be completed by a registered (licensed) or in the case of the USA an accredited veterinarian, or an Official Veterinarian.

If the veterinarian whose name and signature appear on Veterinary Certificate A is not an Official Veterinarian, Veterinary Certificate A must be presented to an Official Veterinarian for signature and stamping (this can be done with Step 19).

Your pet will be required to be free from clinical signs of infectious or contagious diseases, including transmissible venereal tumors (dogs) and external parasites and be fit to travel.

Corrections to Veterinary Certificates will only be accepted if the original entry has been struck through and remains legible. The Official Veterinarian must sign each correction.

STEP 19: COMPLETION OF VETERINARY CERTIFICATE B, SEALING ANIMAL IN THE SHIPPING CONTAINER.   *check once completed* ____
Time frame: After the completion of Veterinary Certificate A, usually on the day of departure.

The following documents must be presented to the Official Veterinarian at this time for signature and stamp (endorsing) and then travel with your pet to Australia.

- The original permit to import (the permit needs to be sighted only)
- The original Veterinary Certificate A.
- The original or copy of the last rabies vaccination certificate.
- The original or copy of the RNATT laboratory report.
- Originals or copies of the Nipah virus laboratory report (Pets from Malaysia only)
- Originals or copies of the general vaccination certificates required in Step 9.
- Originals or copies of the Brucellosis, Ehrlichiosis and Leptospirosis laboratory reports (dogs only).

This Official Veterinarian must also complete, sign and stamp Veterinary Certificate B.

The Official Veterinarian who signs Veterinary Certificate B must record the identification number of the seal on Veterinary Certificate B, and seal your pet into the cage. Under no circumstances must your pet be released from its cage once sealed. Ensure that your pet is prepared for travel before the cage is sealed (see Step 20).

Corrections to Veterinary Certificates will only be accepted if the original entry has been struck through and remains legible. The Official Veterinarian must sign each correction.

STEP 20 CHECK PET IN WITH THE AIRLINE. *check once completed* ____
Time frame: Please check with your airline.

> You must ensure that that there is water available inside the travel cage for your pet to drink during the flight, an external funnel with a hose into a water container fixed inside the cage should be provided, allowing water to be replenished. Sufficient adsorbent bedding (bedding will be destroyed on arrival in Australia) should also be provided. The container should also be marked "Live Animal".
> In most cases your pet will be checked in at the freight terminal, not the passenger terminal.

The original import permit and original Veterinary Certificates A and B must be presented when checking the animal in with the airline, and must travel with your pet to Australia. All laboratory reports and vaccination certificates must also travel with your pet. Laboratory reports and vaccination certificates may be either copies or originals but must bear the original signature and stamp by the Official Veterinarian.

Please make photocopies of all documents. AQIS recommends taping one set of photocopied documents onto the cage while keeping another set with you.

> If, in exceptional circumstances, your pets container must be opened during transit or transhipment it should be resealed and a certificate should be provided by an Official Veterinarian, port authority, or captain of the aircraft detailing the circumstances. <u>Instructions to this effect should be attached to the outside of the container before departure from the port of export.</u>

DOGS AND CATS RETURNING TO AUSTRALIA AFTER LESS THAN 6 MONTHS RESIDENCY IN COUNTRY OF EXPORT

Australian dogs and cats may be eligible to return to Australia with less than six (6) months residency in the country of export, provided the animal has resided continuously in the country since being imported directly from Australia. This concession allows the animals to undergo the minimum period of post-entry quarantine (30 days) on return to Australia. The following additional conditions must also be met.

BEFORE LEAVING AUSTRALIA
  1. Microchip Animal
  Dogs and cats must be identified by a microchip that can be read by an Avidâ, Trovanâ, Destronâ or other ISO compatible reader. The microchip must be implanted prior to, or at the time of rabies vaccination in Australia.
  2. Vaccinate animal against rabies
  Arrange for animal to be vaccinated with an approved inactivated rabies vaccine at least one (1) month and not more than six (6) months prior to leaving Australia. The animal must be at least three (3) months of age to receive this vaccine. Ensure that the microchip number appears on the rabies vaccination certificate.
  3. RNATT prior to leaving Australia.
  Your pet will not be granted permission to return to Australia under this provision unless blood was taken for a RNATT conducted in Australia prior to export and recorded a positive result. See Step 5 for more information. This test should be conducted at least 30 days after the rabies vaccination, your pet's microchip number must appear on the laboratory report.
  4. Follow steps 6-20 on this information sheet.

APPROVED RABIES-FREE COUNTRIES AND TERRITORIES REQUIRING
NO QUARANTINE:
Cocos (Keeling) Islands, New Zealand, Norfolk Island.

APPROVED RABIES-FREE COUNTRIES AND TERRITORIES—MINIMUM
OF 30 DAYS QUARANTINE (Information sheet 2):
Bahrain, Barbados, Cyprus, Falkland Islands, Fiji, French Polynesia, Guam,
Hawaii, the Republic of Ireland, Japan, Malta, Mauritius, New Caledonia,
Norway, Singapore, Sweden, Taiwan, the United Kingdom, Vanuatu.

APPROVED RABIES-FREE ISLAND COUNTRIES AND TERRITORIES—
MINIMUM OF 60 DAYS QUARANTINE (Information sheet 3):
American Samoa, Cook Islands, Federated States of Micronesia, Kiribati,
Papua New Guinea, Solomon Islands, Kingdom of Tonga, Wallis and Futuna,
Western Samoa.

APPROVED RABIES-FREE ISLAND COUNTRIES AND TERRITORIES
WHICH MAY NOT HAVE AN OFFICIAL VETERINARY SERVICE—MINI-
MUM OF 60 DAYS QUARANTINE (Information sheet 3):
Christmas Island, Nauru, Niue, Tuvalu.

APPROVED COUNTRIES AND TERRITORIES RECOGNISED BY THE
AUSTRALIAN GOVERNMENT AS COUNTRIES AND TERRITORIES IN
WHICH DOG-MEDIATED RABIES IS ABSENT OR WELL CONTROLLED—
MINIMUM OF 30 DAYS QUARANTINE & RABIES VACCINATION
(Information sheet 4):
Antigua and Barbuda, Austria, Bahamas, Belgium, Bermuda, British Vir-
gin Islands, Brunei, Canada, Cayman islands, Chile, Croatia, Czech Repub-
lic, Denmark, France, Finland, Germany, Greece, Greenland, Hong Kong,
Hungary, Israel, Italy, Jamaica, Kuwait, Luxembourg, Macau, Peninsular
Malaysia, Netherlands, Netherlands-Antilles and Aruba, Portugal, Puerto Rico,
Reunion, Sabah, Sarawak, Seychelles, South Korea, Spain, St Kitts and Nevis,
St Lucia, St Vincent Grenadin, Saipan, Switzerland (including Liechtenstein),
Trinidad and Tobago, United Arab Emirates, United States of America, US
Virgin Islands, Uruguay, Yugoslavia (including Montenegro Serbia and
Kosovo).

APPROVED COUNTRIES AND TERRITORIES RECOGNISED BY THE
AUSTRALIAN GOVERNMENT AS COUNTRIES AND TERRITORIES IN
WHICH DOG-MEDIATED RABIES IS ENDEMIC (Information sheet 5):

Republic of South Africa—Importation of dogs and cats from non-approved countries can only occur indirectly via an approved country where the animal must be continuously resident for at least the six months immediately prior to export to Australia. The animal is then eligible for import under the conditions that apply to that approved country.

ADDRESSES OF PRINCIPAL VETERINARY OFFICERS (QUARANTINE):
For quarantine at Eastern Creek (NSW) apply to:

Principal Veterinary Officer (Quarantine)
Eastern Creek Animal Quarantine Station
Wallgrove Road
Eastern Creek, NSW 2766
Telephone: (02) 9832 4025
Facsimile: (02) 9832 1532

For quarantine at Byford (WA) apply to:

Principal Veterinary Officer (Quarantine)
Byford Animal Quarantine Station
P.O. Box 61
Byford, WA 6201
Telephone: (08) 9525 1763
Facsimile (08) 9526 2199

For quarantine at Spotswood (Vic.) apply to:

Principal Veterinary Officer (Quarantine)
Spotswood Animal Quarantine Station
P.O. Box 300Newport, Victoria 3015
Telephone (03) 9391 1627
Facsimile (03) 9391 0860

ANIMAL QUARANTINE FEE SCHEDULE FOR DOGS AND CATS:
The application fee is payable at the time your application is forwarded to AQIS. All other fees must be paid prior to release of animal from quarantine. An invoice detailing quarantine costs is generated upon the arrival of your pet after arrival at the quarantine station and will be forwarded to you.

1. Lodgement of an application form—$60.00

2. Lodgement of a quarantine entry form—$12.00
3. Performance of a service for which a fee is not specified elsewhere in this schedule.
   - other (including examination of live animals)—$68.00 for the first ½ hour or part thereof for each officer performing the service and thereafter $34.00 per ¼ hour or part thereof for each officer performing the service
4. Documentation clearance—$30.00 per ¼ hour or part thereof for each officer performing the service
5. Conveyance from port of arrival to the quarantine station
   - business hours—$95.00 per importer per service
   - outside hours—$120.00 per importer per service
6. Accommodation and management of animals at quarantine station
   - first cat (6 weeks or more old)—$12.00 per day
   - first dog (6 weeks or more old)—$16.00 per day
   - additional cat (6 weeks or more old)—$9.00   per day
   - additional dog (6 weeks or more old)—$11.00 per day
   - a bitch that whelps during quarantine—$400.00 max 7 hours supervision plus $19.00 each additional hour plus the daily rate ($5.00 per day per pup up until the age of 6 weeks and thereafter $11.00 per day)
   - a cat that gives birth during quarantine—$300.00 plus the daily rate
7. Bordetella (kennel cough) vaccination if required. At owners expense.
   - Veterinary supplies and treatment at cost.

NB: Charges are valid at 16 August 1999 and are subject to change.

Australian Quarantine Contact Telephone Numbers—Ports

QUEENSLAND

Thursday Island	(07) 4069 1185
Weipa	(07) 4069 7380
Cairns	(07) 4030 7800
Townsville	(07) 4722 2684
Mackay	(07) 4957 6388
Bundaberg	(07) 4152 2511
Gladstone	(07) 4972 0038
Brisbane	(07) 3246 8754

NEW SOUTH WALES

Coffs Harbour	(02) 6652 5599
Newcastle	(02) 4962 4452
Sydney	(02) 9247 5644
Port Kembla	(02) 4274 4791
Alstonville (Yamba)	(02) 6622 7333
Eden	(02) 6496 1667
Lord Howe Island	(02) 6563 2199

VICTORIA

Melbourne	(03) 9246 6827
Geelong	(03) 5222 5855
Portland	(03) 5523 3077

TASMANIA

Hobart	(03) 6233 3528
Launceston	(03) 6336 2174
Burnie	(03) 6434 6265

SOUTH AUSTRALIA

All Ports	(08) 8305 9752

NORTHERN TERRITORY

Darwin	(08) 8999 2109
Gove- Nhulunbuy	(08) 8997 1136
Cocos (Keeling) Islands	(08) 9162 6584

WESTERN AUSTRALIA

Esperance	(08) 9071 3011
Albany	(08) 9841 4388
Bunbury	(08) 9780 6213
Fremantle	(08) 9311 5353
Geraldton	(08) 9921 5014
Port Headland	(08) 9173 2135
Karratha/Dampier/ Walcott	(08) 9185 2865
Broome	(08) 9192 1579
Perth	(08) 9311 5331
Wyndham	(08) 9168 1166

APPLICATION FORM

FOR THE IMPORTATION OF CATS AND DOGS INTO AUSTRALIA

- You must complete one of these forms for each cat or dog to be imported

- The completed form/s **and fee of $60** Australian dollars per application must be sent to the quarantine station of your choice. If sending a cheque with your application it should be posted, if paying by credit card you may post or fax your application to us. Cheques are payable to the "Collector of Public Monies-AQIS" - Amex, Visa, Matercard and Bankcard are also accepted.

SECTIONS 1, 2, 3, 4 and 5 must be completed by all applicants.

SECTION 6 should only be completed if importing more than one animal.

SECTION 7 must be completed if importing a dog from a category 4 country (where dog-mediated rabies is absent or well controlled) or South Africa. An OFFICIAL VETERINARIAN of the country of export must complete this section. Do not fill out section 7 if you are importing a cat or dog from a category 1,2 or 3 country.

Please either type or write clearly in BLOCK letters.

---

1. Country of origin

The country of origin of your cat or dog:..

Date of application:..Expected date of export:................................

---

2. Importer details

Details of IMPORTER /Owner or Representative in Australia:

Mr/Mrs/Ms:...(surname)...(given name)

Address:...

....

....AUSTRALIA.   E-mail..

Telephone:(Home)....................................(Work) ....Fax:......................................

---

3. Exporter details

Details of the EXPORTER / owner / representative in the country of origin:

Mr/ Mrs/ Ms:...…...................(surname)...(giv
name)

Address:...

....

....…..........E-mail:...

Telephone:(Home)................................(Work) .... Fax:..
Please include country codes and area codes.

Please either type or write clearly in BLOCK letters. Where applicable, please tick the relevant box ☑.

4. Description of animal	
Animal's name:	Age or date of birth(day/month/year): ....
Species: Dog ☐ Cat ☐	Sex: Male (entire) ☐ Male de-sexed ☐ Female (entire) ☐ Female de-sexed ☐

Breed (for mixed breed animals, indicate the breed/s which the animal most closely resembles):

....

Pregnancy: Will the animal be pregnant on arrival in Australia?

No ☐ Yes ☐ Expected date of birth (day/month/year)...

5. Microchip details AQIS can not issue a permit to import if this section is not completed.	
Microchip number:	Microchip reader type: Avid ☐ Destron ☐ Trovan ☐ Other ISO Compatible:........................

6. Animals sharing quarantine accommodation. Please complete this section if you are intending to import more than one animal. Shared accommodation will only be granted for animals of the same species.

Do you want this cat/dog to share quarantine accommodation with another pet owned by you?

No ☐

Yes ☐ Name, microchip number and species of other animal: ....

....

Postal and fax details of our quarantine stations

Sydney - New South Wales	Melbourne - Victoria -	Perth - Western Australia
Eastern Creek Animal Quarantine Station 60 Wallgrove Rd Eastern Creek NSW 2766 Fax: (612) 9832 1532	Spotswood Animal Quarantine Station PO Box 300 Newport VIC 3015 Fax: (613) 9391 0860	Byford Animal Quarantine Station PO Box 61 Byford WA 6201 Fax: (618) 9526 2199

7. Rabies vaccination and Rabies Neutralising Antibody Titre Testing (RNATT).
This section must completed when importing animals from a category 4 country or South Africa.

THIS SECTION MUST BE COMPLETED, SIGNED AND STAMPED BY <u>AN OFFICIAL VETERINARIAN</u> OF THE COUNTRY OF EXPORT. A PERMIT TO IMPORT WILL NOT BE IS IF ANY PART OF THIS SECTION IS BLANK. [A copy of the RNATT must be attached]

I ....(Name of Official Veterinaria

....(Address of Official Veterinaria

declare that I have sighted the rabies vaccination certificate and the RNATT report.

- The date of last rabies vaccination is recorded as:
  ....

- The animals age at last rabies vaccination
  was:..

- The laboratory reporting the RNATT is government-approved: Yes ☐
- Name and address of approved laboratory:...
  ....

- The microchip number that appears on the RNATT report is:...

- Blood samples taken for RNATT were drawn on:...(dd/mm/yy)

- The RNATT result is recorded as:..........................International Units/ml in animal's serum
  (the RNATT result must be at least 0.5IU/ml)

....
Signature of Official Veterinarian   **Stamp of Official**
Veterinarian
Faxed applications must bear the stamp of the Official Veterinarian rather than a raised se

DECLARATION

I declare that this animal is not a Pitbull Terrier or American Pitbull Terrier or Fila Brasileiro or Dogo Argentino or Japanese Tosa. Also, the animal is not a domestic animal hybrid such as a wolf or bengal cat having any pure-bred ancestor less than 5th generations away.

I declare that to the best of my knowledge and belief all the above information is true and correct

....
(Signature and printed name of applicant)

Date:.......................

AQIS
protecting our way of life

Please complete the following details if you are paying by credit card

For details of goods and services please refer to the attached application for

Amount paid:	☐	Card No:	☐☐☐☐☐☐☐☐☐☐☐☐☐☐☐☐☐☐

Please debit my:	☐ Bankcard	Valid dates:	☐ to ☐

☐ **MasterCard**

☐ **Visa**

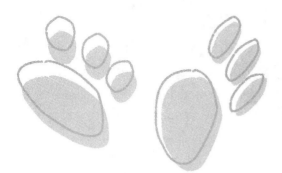

Bibliography

AAA . *Traveling With Your Pet, 3rd edition*. Heathrow, Florida: AAA Publishing, 2001.

Brotman, Eric, Ph D. *How to Toilet Train Your Cat: The Education of Mango*. San Fernando, California: Bird Brain Press, Inc, 2000.

Graham, Robin, and Derek Gill (contributor) Dove: *The Boy Who Sailed Around the World Alone*. Harper Collins,1991

Hays, David and Daniel(contributor). *My Old Man and the Sea: A Father and Son Sail Around Cape Horn*. Harper Collins, 1995, Algonquin (paperback) 1996

Kunkel, Paul. *How to Toilet Train Your Cat: 21 Days to a Litter-Free Home*. New York: Workman Publishing, 1991.

Shojai, Amy D., DVM. *First- Aid Companion for Dogs and Cats*. USA: Rodale Inc, 2001.

Simon, Alvah. *North to the Night, A Year in the Arctic Ice*. Camden, Maine: International Marine/McGraw-Hill, 1999. And Broadway Books, soft cover edition.

Smith, Marjorie L., MD. *You Can Teach Your Dog to Eliminate on Command*. Port Washington, Wisconsin: Seaworthy Publications, Inc., 2003.

Index

About the Author

A native Californian, **Diana Jessie** is a sailor, writer, and lecturer. She contributes to national magazines including *Sail, Cruising World, Yachting, Blue Water Sailing*, and *Ocean Navigator*. Her column, "Realistic Cruising," has appeared monthly in Puget Sound's *48⁰North* for over a decade. Her first book, *The Cruising Woman's Advisor*, explored new territory describing the needs and expectations of women. Twice she has been awarded the Mary Grandin Trophy by St. Francis Yacht Club for outstanding contributions to cruising by a woman. This book *Cruising with Your Four-Footed Friends* explores the basics of having your favorite cat or dog aboard your boat. She is a member of the American Society of Journalists and Authors and Boating Writers International. She lives with her husband and cat aboard their 48' sailboat on San Francisco Bay.